Table of Contents

Introduction

The terrorist attacks on 9/11 horrified the world and served as the catalyst for two major wars in the first decade of the 21st Century. In addition, the attacks underscored the vulnerability of U.S. homeland security due to its porous borders and open society. To counter the threats against the nation, U.S. policy-makers created the Department of Homeland Security (DHS) and its military counter-part, U.S. Northern Command (USNORTHCOM or NORTHCOM).[1] Of the two organizations, the former is responsible for homeland security, and the latter is responsible for homeland defense. Working in coordination, these two organizations represented a whole of government approach to providing for the security and defense of the United States.

The DHS defines homeland security differently than the U.S. military.[2] To add clarification, this assessment uses the U.S. military doctrinal definition of homeland security, which describes it as, "A concerted national effort to prevent terrorist attacks within the United States; reduce America's vulnerability to terrorism, major disasters, and other emergencies; and minimize the damage and recover from attacks, major disasters, and other emergencies that occur."[3] The definition serves as a foundation for framing problems associated with homeland security by clearly delineating that the focus of effort is within the borders of the United States; where the Department of Defense (DOD) is in support of civil authorities.

---

[1] United States Northern Command, About USNORTHCOM, http://www.northcom.mil/About/index.html (accessed February 6, 2012); U.S. Department of Homeland Security, Creation of the Department of Homeland Security, http://www.dhs.gov/xabout/history/gc_1297963906741.shtml.

[2] U.S. Department of Homeland Security, *Quadrennial Homeland Security Review Report: A Strategic Framework for a Secure Homeland* (Washington, DC: U.S. Department of Homeland Security, February, 2010), 13. The QHSRR defines homeland security as a "concerted national effort to ensure a homeland that is safe, secure, and resilient against terrorism and other hazards where American interests, aspirations, and way of life can thrive."

[3] U.S. Department of Defense, *Department of Defense Dictionary of Military and Associated Terms,* JP 1-0 (Washington, DC: Department of Defense, April 12, 2001 (as amended through April, 2010), 214.

1

Conversely, homeland defense is, "The protection of United States sovereignty, territory, domestic population, and critical defense infrastructure against external threats and aggression or other threats as directed by the President."[4] A vital part of national defense strategy, homeland defense serves as one layer in the layered defense of the nation.[5] This layer, unlike homeland security, focuses on threats outside the nation's borders and is the responsibility of the DOD.

Even with this layered approach, threats continue to emerge that pose significant danger to national security. At the forefront of these threats is Al Qaeda's continued aim of conducting a massive attack on U.S. soil and a significant increase of violence caused by Mexican-based Transnational Criminal Organizations (TCO) over control of ungoverned areas along the U.S.-Mexico Border.[6] Although the recent death of Osama Bin Laden and increased counterdrug efforts under the Mérida Initiative show that U.S. led efforts are producing positive results against violent extremist and TCOs; these successes, when placed in a greater context, are minimal and insufficient to counter growing national security threats.[7] For example, in 2009 federal law enforcement agencies seized about 1.5 million kilograms of illicit drugs passing through the

---

[4] *Department of Defense Dictionary of Military and Associated Term*, 214.

[5] U.S. Department of Defense, *2008 National Defense Strategy* (Washington DC: Office of the Secretary of Defense, June 2008), 6.

[6] President, *National Strategy for Counterterrorism* (Washington, DC: June 2011), 3, http://www.whitehouse.gov/sites/default/files/counterterrorism_strategy.pdf (accessed February 14, 2012); Kristin Finklea, William Krouse and Marc Rosenblum, *Southwest Border Violence: Issues in Identifying and Measuring Spillover Violence*, CRS Report for Congress R41075 (Washington, DC: Congressional Research Service, June 9, 2011), 2, http://www fas.org/sgp/crs/homesec/R41075.pdf (accessed September 15, 2011).

[7] Clare Ribando Seelke and Kristin M. Finklea, *U.S.-Mexican Security Cooperation: The Mérida Initiative and Beyond*, CRS Report for Congress R41349 (Washington, DC: Congressional Research Service, August 15, 2011), 30, http://www.fas.org/sgp/crs/row/R41349.pdf (accessed February March 1, 2012). The Mérida Initiative is a "counterdrug and anticrime assistance package for Mexico and Central America" created by President G.W. Bush's administration in 2007.

Southwest Border. This represented, "... no more than 9 percent of the $6 to 7 billion in total proceeds that Mexican [TCOs] derive from the United States each year."[8]

The TCOs ninety percent success rate of smuggling illegal narcotics into the country provides an attractive way for extremist groups to infiltrate men and material into the nation. Standing on the frontline against this future threat is the Customs and Border Protection (CBP) and Immigration and Customs Enforcement (ICE); supported by NORTHCOM's Joint Task Force – North (JTF-North). Although the dedicated men and women of ICE, CBP, and JTF-North risk their lives daily to protect the nation's border, a meager ten percent success rate highlights that gaps in capability exist within the three organizations that prevent it from effectively controlling cross-border illicit trafficking.

Using the U.S. Army Capabilities-Based Assessment model as a guide, the following analysis examines the current operational capabilities of ICE, CBP, and USNORTHCOM. The analysis then highlights the capabilities required to combat current and future threats along the Southwest Border and identifies the gaps between existing and required capabilities. From this gap analysis, this study proposes a set of solutions to fill these capability shortfalls leveraging existing DOD capabilities. While not all-inclusive, these solutions provide the U.S. government with a framework to build DHS capacity along the Southwest border and better counter the threats of growing instability within Mexico.

The U.S. Army Capabilities Based Assessment model is a three-phased approach to, "... identif[y] capability needs and gaps and [and to] recommend non-materiel or materiel approaches

---

[8] David A. Shirk, "Transnational Crime, U.S. Border Security, and the War on Drugs in Mexico," (Delivered to the House of Representatives Sub-Committee on Oversight, Investigations, and Management, Chairman: Hon. Michael McCaul, March 31, 2011), http://homeland house.gov/sites/homeland house.gov/ files/Testimony%20Shirk.pdf (accessed March 21, 2012).

to address gaps."[9] Phase one of the model is the Functional Area Analysis, which describes the problem, scenario, and required capabilities. Phase two, the Functional Needs Analysis, describes current capabilities and capability gaps. Lastly, phase three of the model, the Functional Solutions Analysis, identifies potential solutions through changes in Doctrine, Organization, Training, Material, Leadership and Education, Personnel, and/or Facilities (DOTMLPF).[10]

Cooperation between the U.S. military and civil law enforcement agencies has existed throughout the nation's history. Chapter one provides the evolution of civil-military cooperation; beginning with operations to eradicate Klu Klux Klan influence in the southern states following the civil war, and ending with the attacks on 9/11. This historical context highlights significant paradigm shifts in the environment that resulted in separate homeland security and homeland defense lines of effort that today defines the U.S. approach to national security.[11]

The attacks on 9/11 underscored the nation's vulnerability to attack from extremist groups operating both within and outside U.S. borders. Using the Functional Area Analysis phase of the CBA model as a guide, chapter two defines threats to homeland security that emerged post-9/11, the current threat, future threat, and the nation's response post-9/11 through today. This holistic description of the operational environment highlights the problem facing current U.S. military and civilian law enforcement agencies in countering a potential alignment between the strategic aims of the TCOs and Al Qaeda. If aligned, these groups pose an even greater threat to U.S. national security.

---

[9] U.S. Department of the Army, *TRADOC Capabilities-Based Assessment (CBA) Version 3.1* (Fort Monroe, VA: Training and Doctrine Command, May 10, 2010), 3.

[10] *TRADOC Capabilities-Based Assessment (CBA) Version 3.1*, 5, L-3.

[11] U.S. Department of the Army, *The Operations Process*, FM 5-0 (Washington, DC: U.S. Department of the Army, March 2010), 2-17. "Lines of effort link multiple tasks with goal-oriented objectives that focus efforts toward establishing end state conditions."

To arm NORTHCOM, CBP, and ICE with the capabilities necessary for meeting the threat posed by future narco-trafficking organizations and extremist groups, the third chapter assesses current NORTHCOM, CBP, and ICE capabilities, the required capabilities of these organizations, gaps in existing versus required capabilities, and recommended solutions to fill these gaps. Representing phase two and three of the CBA model, this study limits its recommended solutions to changes within the Doctrine, Training, Organization areas of DOTMLPF, and changes in governmental policy. Focusing on DOT/policy gives strategic leaders options that do not require development of new technologies or increase overall end strength of both DOD and DHS.

Since the creation of DHS and NORTHCOM, both the U.S. military and civilian law enforcement organizations have gained critical experience in the fight against terrorism both inside and outside the borders of the United States. At the same time, additional threats to national security have developed which reinforce the need for increased collaboration between governmental agencies and the U.S. military in the homeland. Transnational criminal organizations (TCOs) operating on and through the nation's southern border underscores this point. Combining the experience and capabilities of a battle hardened joint force and competent domestic law enforcement agencies serves as a powerful tool to counter these emerging threats.

Evolution of U.S. Homeland Security and Defense

Prior to the Spanish-American War, the U.S. military and federal law enforcement agencies worked hand in hand to provide homeland security. Following the defeat of the Confederate Army, the Klu Klux Klan emerged in the southern states as a threat to national security by disrupting the electoral process through intimidation. Labeled a terrorist organization

by the federal government, Congress took action because the Klu Klux Klan was, "…
[Conspiring] to prevent an act of Congress."[12] The response to this threat was the deployment of
U.S. military units into the southern states to find, capture, and bring to justice members of the
Klu Klux Klan. However, the U.S. military soon realized they were not suited for investigating
and finding individuals spread across vast stretches of land amongst a sympathetic population.
Additionally, the local police in the south were not trustworthy because of the Klan's influence
over them.[13]

The force needed for dismantling the Klu Klux Klan in the south, required men who had
investigative skills and experience in managing intelligence from human sources, possessed
loyalties to an institution outside of southern influence, and the authority to execute criminal
justice activities. The U.S. government found these men in the already established U.S. Secret
Service (USSS). In one of the first examples of U.S. federal law enforcement and military
cooperation, the addition of the USSS in the south to defeat the national threat posed by the Klu
Klux Klan was a resounding success. By the end of 1872, the campaign defeated the Klu Klux
Klan through a hailstorm of federal convictions and effectively ended the organization's influence
in the south.[14]

The War with Spain in 1898 serves as a point of departure from the cooperative U.S.
military-federal law enforcement approach to homeland security. With a more global view, and
the realization that its porous borders were vulnerable, policy-makers had to "…develop and
refine American domestic legal, defense and policing institutions…" to counter emerging threats

---

[12] Rhodri Jeffreys-Jones, *The FBI: A History* (New Haven, CT: Yale University Press, 2007), 21.

[13] Wyn Craig Wade, *The Fiery Cross: The Klu Klux Klan in America* (London: Simon and Schuster, 1987), 83-84.

[14] Jeffreys-Jones, *The FBI: A History*, 30. Although there was a resurgence of Klu Klux Klan activities after 1872, this was due to less focus on the subject by the U.S. government in the later years.

6

to the nation.[15] Prior to the war, the U.S. focused on defending against threats to its natural

borders with its military. However, the defeat of Spain brought new responsibilities to the U.S.;

namely the Philippines. With its newfound responsibility to provide for the protection of a people

outside the continental United States, it was necessary to re-orient the U.S. military from a mainly

defensive force to an expeditionary force.[16] This new mission created a gap in the security of the

nation.

To ensure the continued security of the nation, policy-makers sought a strategy that

guaranteed U.S. military surge capacity for expeditionary operations while also maintaining the

capacity to defend the homeland.[17] The solution to this problem was federalizing the U.S.

National Guard (USNG). Federalization of the USNG came into being through the Dick Act,

named for its creator Major General Charles Dick, which became law on January 21, 1903.[18] The

new law improved state National Guard programs through standardized training (supervised by

the regular army), improved equipment, and federal funding. In addition, Section 4 of the law

stated:

> That whenever the United is invaded, or in danger of invasion from any foreign nation or
> of rebellion against the authority of the Government of the United States, or the President
> is unable, with other forces at his command, to execute the laws of the Union in any part
> thereof, it shall be lawful for the President to call forth, for a period not exceeding nine
> months, such number of the militia of the State or of the States or Territories or of the
> District of Columbia as he may deem necessary to repel such invasion, suppress such

---

[15] Tom Lansford, Robert J. Pauly, Jr., and Jack Covarrubias, *To Protect and Defend: US Homeland Security Policy* (Burlington, VT: Ashgate Publishing Company, 2006), 43.

[16] Lansford, Pauly, Jr., and Covarrubias, *To Protect and Defend: US Homeland Security Policy*, 43-44.

[17] Ibid.

[18] John K. Mahon, *History of the Militia and the National Guard* (New York: Macmillan Publishing Company, 1983), 139. The original name of the Dick Act of 1903 was the Militia Act of 1903.

rebellion, or to enable him to execute such laws, and to issue his orders for that purpose to such officers of the militia as he may think proper.[19]

Despite the improvements to the USNG because of the Dick Act, the law assumed that the USNG would feed future wartime armies through trained volunteers from its ranks.[20] Therefore, there was no system to ensure unit cohesion during times of need. As a result, leaders in Washington viewed USNG units as unreliable because of their disorganization and primary allegiance to state governors.[21] The next evolution in the USNG federalization sought to correct this oversight.

Over the next 12 years, two major additions to the Dick Act of 1903 solidified the solution to the problem of domestic security as the U.S. began its climb to global dominance. The first was a law passed by Congress in May 1908, and the second was the National Defense Act of 1916. The former removed the constraint of nine-month service of the USNG stated in the Dick Act and allowed the President of the United States to dictate the length of service based on the threat. The latter created the U.S. Army Reserves, the Reserve Officer Training Corps (ROTC), and "…categorically stated that the National Guard was an integral part of the [U.S.] Army of the United States when in federal service."[22] In combination, the Dick Act of 1903, term of service law of May 1908, and the National Defense Act of 1916 ensured a trained pool of military aged males and gave more federal control over the USNG. However, with national security strategy focusing more and more outside the borders of the U.S., an additional gap in homeland security surfaced that required an internal law enforcement solution.

---

[19] United States and John A. Mallory, "The Militia," in *Compiled Statutes of the United States: Supplement 1903* (St. Paul, MN: West Publishing Company, 1903), 133-134 http://books.google.com/ (accessed December 14, 2011).

[20] Mahon, *History of the Militia and the National Guard*, 140.

[21] Mahon, *History of the Militia and the National Guard*, 142.

[22] Ibid., 148.

With the U.S. military focused outside of the borders of the nation, a single layer approach to homeland security and defense was no longer capable of combating the threats to the nation. The Federal Bureau of Investigation (FBI) added the internal security layer to the U.S. homeland security and defense approach. With the creation of the FBI in 1908, the U.S. possessed the military and law enforcement organizations it needed for a multi-layered approach to homeland security.[23] However, the onset of World War I (WWI) set the conditions for an unprecedented response by the U.S. government to counter the perceived threats to the homeland.

In August 1914, war broke out in Europe that catapulted the world into one of the bloodiest conflicts known to man. WWI forced the U.S. to enter unknown territory in homeland security posed by a war that seemed uncontrollable. American fears began to escalate, "fueled by [an] influx of immigrants, the [rise] of [militant] labor unions, growth in [communist and socialist] political groups, widespread opposition to the [U.S.] getting involved in [WWI], and strong opposition to [a] draft."[24] Although the war brought about fears on a national scale, not all were without warrant.

German intelligence operatives were active within the nation's borders prior to the U.S. entering the war in 1917. These activities included the introduction of German propaganda into the U.S., encouraging labor disputes, and the planning of bombing attacks throughout the country. The plots, uncovered by the USSS, indicated two things to the government: the U.S. had an existing threat to homeland security and an inadequate counter-intelligence capability to counter

---

[23] Federal Bureau of Investigation, "A Brief History of the FBI," http://www.fbi.gov/about-us/history/brief-history (accessed March 6, 2012).

[24] Bruce Maxwell, *Homeland Security: A Documentary History* (Washington, DC: CQ Press, 2004), 17.

that threat. The initial response, executed by the government in 1916, empowered the FBI to conduct noncriminal investigations under the direction of the U.S. Attorney General.[25]

Beginning in 1917, President Woodrow Wilson developed more robust policies to counter the threats to homeland security. Two of these policies, The Espionage Act of 1917 and the Sedition Act of 1918, captured this periods approach to homeland security and defense. The Espionage Act of 1917 outlawed interfering with any aspect of the U.S. military during times of war by stating,

> Whoever, when the United States is at war, shall willfully…cause or attempt to cause insubordination, disloyalty, mutiny, or refusal of duty, in the military or naval forces of the United States, or shall willfully obstruct the recruiting or enlistment service of the United States, to the injury of the service or of the United States, shall be punished by a fine of not more than $10,000 or imprisonment for not more than twenty years or both.[26]

The Sedition Act of 1918 broadened the laws set out in the Espionage Act of 1917 by including not only the U.S. military but also the U.S. government. It states,

> Whoever, when the United States is at war…shall willfully utter, print, write, or publish any disloyal, profane, scurrilous, or abusive language about the form of government of the United States, or the flag of the United States, or the military or naval forces of the United States…and whoever shall willfully advocate, teach, defend, or suggest the doing of any of the acts or things in this section…shall be punished by a fine of not more than $10,000 or imprisonment for not more than twenty years, or both.[27]

Both laws sought to limit anti-war and anti-American sentiments and gave further authority to the executive branch of the government to execute the laws.

By the end of WWI, the FBI grew from a mere nine agents in 1908 to more than 225 agents in 1918. Not only did manpower increase, but their budget increased as well; tripling from

---

[25] Jeffreys-Jones, *The FBI: A History*, 67-69.

[26] John Augustus Lapp, *Supplement to 1917, to Lapp's Important Federal Laws* (Indianapolis, IN: B.F. Bowen & Company, 1917), 73-74, http://books.google.com/books/ (accessed December 14, 2011).

[27] Maxwell, *Homeland Security: A Documentary History*, 24.

10

1914 to 1918.[28] All told, the combination of increased manpower, resources, and authority resulted in the internment of over 2300 illegal aliens and thousands of arrests of draft dodgers, radicals, and other "suspicious" people of interest.[29]

During the inter-war period, the FBI's authority and resources continued to grow while the U.S. military drastically reduced its forces. Aiding in the growth of the FBI was a series of threats to homeland security ranging from the fear of communist infiltrations of American institutions to organized crime syndicates during the period of Prohibition.[30] However, as a new war began to escalate in Europe, a new set of threats to the security of the nation surfaced which required a more synergistic relationship between the military and the FBI.[31]

Prior to the U.S. entering WWII, intelligence collection responsibilities fell on the U.S. military and the FBI. The military was responsible for collection outside the borders of the U.S., and the FBI was responsible for counterespionage internal to the nation and its territories.[32] The stove-piped system required coordination between the two organizations to provide the overall intelligence picture necessary for homeland security and defense. However, cultural differences and power struggles made coordination between the military and FBI problematic, which led to missed opportunities and misguided decisions.[33]

---

[28] Jeffreys-Jones, *The FBI: A History*, 62, 72. The FBIs budget in 1914 was $475,000. This increased to $1,101,486 by 1918.

[29] Maxwell, *Homeland Security: A Documentary History*, 18.

[30] Lansford, Pauly, Jr., and Covarrubias, *To Protect and Defend: US Homeland Security Policy*, 45-46.

[31] Ibid., 46.

[32] Jeffreys-Jones, *The FBI: A History,* 107-108.

[33] Ibid., 100-119.

One of these misguided decisions, which serves as an example of an extreme response to a perceived threat to homeland security, is the internment of Japanese-Americans during WWII. Beginning with the attacks at Pearl Harbor, heightened tensions between the Japanese-American community and the inhabitants of the bulk of the western states began to inflame. By 1942, Washington, Oregon, California, and a portion of Arizona became a "military area" where President Roosevelt ordered the relocation of all persons of "Japanese lineage" into internment facilities. In total, over 100,000 Japanese-Americans settled into the internment camps established by the Western Defense Command. Almost one-third never returned to their homes after their release at war's end.[34]

With the lessons from WWII still fresh on policy-makers' minds, and the onset of the Cold War, the stage was set for massive reforms to the U.S. approach to homeland security and defense. In his book *A History of the American People*, Paul Johnson asserts, "What was now required, from America, as it was committed to a global strategy of military, diplomatic, and economic outreach, were institutional and structural changes."[35] This change came from the Truman administration with the enactment of the 1947 National Security Act, which created the DOD, Central Intelligence Agency (CIA), and the National Security Council (NSC).[36]

The National Security Act of 1947 serves as another departure point in the approach to homeland security and defense. Prior to WWII, the U.S. government focused most of its efforts on homeland security, and less emphasis on homeland defense. However, the rising threat posed

---

[34] U.S. National Archives, "The War Relocation Authority & the Incarceration of Japanese-Americans during WWII," http://www.trumanlibrary.org/whistlestop/study_collections /japanese_internment/1942.htm http://www.archives.gov/research/military/vietnam-war/casualty-statistics.html (accessed March 7, 2012).

[35] Paul Johnson, *A History of the American People* (New York: Harper Collins Publishers, 1997), 812.

[36] Johnson, *A History of the American People*, 812.

by the Union of Soviet Socialist Republics (USSR), catapulted homeland defense to the top of the agenda. The DOD emerged as the dominant agency within the government, because the organization provided the means to contain communist expansionism and deter a nuclear war.[37] Until the collapse of the USSR, beginning in 1989, the combined strategies of containment and deterrence served as the centerpiece of security policy for all post-WWII administrations.

The military approach to homeland defense during the Cold War, referred to as the "Transoceanic Era" by Krepenevich and Work, is best described as, "…[the U.S. adoption of a Garrison Posture] which saw the basing of large numbers of combat troops on foreign soil."[38] Following WWII, for the first time in the nation's history, the U.S. government possessed a large standing peacetime military capable of projecting power outside its borders to protect national interests. The forward based military created to contain and deter Soviet expansionism and nuclear attack, solidified the role of the DOD as the prominent primary means for providing defense-in-depth. Crucial to the defense-in-depth approach, and further evidence of shift in U.S military domination over homeland security and defense, was the establishment of the North American Treaty Organization (NATO) in the spring of 1949. Responsible for collective defense against the USSR, NATO remained the primary organization for homeland defense efforts for the next 40 years.

During this period, federal law enforcement agencies played a secondary role in homeland security. Confident that the DOD and organizations such as NATO would provide the

---

[37] Everett Carl Dollman, *Pure Strategy: Power and Principles in the Space and Information Age* (New York: Frank Cass-Taylor & Francis, 2005), 36.

[38] Andrew Krepinevich and Robert O. Work, *A New US Global Defense Posture for the Second Transoceanic Era* (Washington, DC: Center for Strategic and Budgetary Assessments, 2007), i, http://www.csbaonline.org/wp-content/uploads/2011/02/2007.04.20-New-Global-Defense-Posture.pdf (accessed November 30, 2011).

necessary layers to the defense of the nation, federal law enforcement agencies reverted to a pre-WWII role of counter-espionage and crime. However, with the outbreak of the Vietnam War, federal law enforcement found itself dealing with internal anti-war movements. Viewed as communists by President Johnson's administration, federal law enforcement agencies began to investigate the various college-based movements across the country. In the end, the FBI determined the anti-war protest groups were not communist sympathizers.[39]

As the Vietnam War era ended, and a new decade descended on the U.S., President Ronald Reagan instilled new vigor in the defeat of communist expansionism and homeland defense. As Paul Johnson notes in his book, *A History of the American People*, President Reagan, "…believed that Russia was a fundamentally flawed power economically…[Russia's] will to match the West in global defense would eventually falter and crack…"[40] Doubling the U.S. national defense budget between 1981 and 1988, President Reagan set conditions for a rebirth of the post-Vietnam military.[41] The reinvigoration to military spending resulted in an anti-ballistic missile shield known as the Strategic Defense Initiative, rapid deployment forces, shipped based cruise missiles, and the Stealth bomber.[42] By the end of Reagan's presidency, the U.S. possessed the most powerful and technologically advanced military in the world.

The new U.S. war machine proved itself against the Iraqi army in the first months of 1991. Operation Desert Storm took 42 days, including the air and land campaign, and

---

[39] Jeffreys-Jones, *The FBI: A History*, 173.

[40] Johnson, *A History of the American People*, 926-927.

[41] President, Budget, "Historical Tables," *Budget of the United States Government, Fiscal Year 2005* (Washington, DC: Government Printing Office, 2004), 55-56, http://www.gpoaccess.gov/usbudget/fy05/pd /hist.pdf (accessed December 12, 2011).

[42] Johnson, *A History of the American People*, 926-928.

14

successfully ousted Saddam Hussein's army from Kuwait.[43] During this same timeframe, the

Soviet Union ceased to exist and with it the Cold War. These two events solidified the U.S. as the

world's sole super-power and with it a sense of invulnerability. However, it also marked the

beginning of a period of uncertainty regarding threats to the nation.

During this period of uncertainty, President Bill Clinton took a different approach to

homeland security and defense. His approach to homeland security and defense, as outlined in the

1995 edition of the National Security Strategy, focused on engagement and enlargement.[44] This

approach included viewing terrorism as a legal vice military matter. With this strategy, President

Clinton sought to, "…fully exploit all available legal mechanisms to punish international

terrorists."[45] For example, the 1993 bombing of the World Trade Center and the 2000 attack on

the USS Cole, resulted in FBI led criminal investigations. When President Clinton did take

military action, he utilized the hi-tech weaponry developed under the Reagan administration and

later showcased in Desert Storm. [46]

Since the end of the Civil War, the nation's approach to homeland security and defense

has continually evolved. Initially, the U.S. military provided both homeland security and defense

for the nation. After the Civil War, as new threats emerged, it became evident that the U.S.

military no longer possessed all of the capabilities necessary for the combined security and

---

[43] Richard M. Swain, *Lucky War: Third Army in Desert Storm* (Washington, DC: U.S. Army Center of Military History, 1997), 358-359. The air campaign began on January 17, 1991 and cessation of offensive actions began on February 28, 1991.

[44] President, *National Security Strategy 1995* (Washington, DC: February 1995), 2, http://www.au.af mil /au/awc/awcgate/nss/nss-95.pdf (accessed December 13, 2011).

[45] President, *National Security Strategy 1995*, 10.

[46] Lansford, Pauly, Jr., and Covarrubias, *To Protect and Defend: US Homeland Security Policy*, 50-54. President Clinton used cruise-missile strikes in response to the bombings of the U.S. Embassies in 1998.

defense of the nation. Cooperating with federal law enforcement agencies proved decisive in defeating internal threats to homeland security prior to the Spanish American War. As the U.S. became a global power, the emphasis for expeditionary and projected power became the impetus of protecting the nation. As the U.S. military began to focus efforts outside the borders of the U.S., the emphasis on homeland security and defense fluctuated based on major conflicts: during peace the emphasis was on homeland security; during war the emphasis was on homeland defense. However, during the Cold War, organizations responsible for homeland security began to focus more and more on criminal activity as opposed to threats to the overall security of the nation.

The over-shadowing post-Vietnam military revival, led by President Reagan, only reinforced the military dominated approach to homeland security and defense. The defeat of the Iraqi army and end of the Cold War in 1991 reinforced the confidence in the approach of the past 50 years. This confidence bled over into the Clinton administration, and after 10 years of relative stability, the nation's institutions became reliant on the technologically advanced and rapid-deployable military to provide for the safety of the nation. This false sense of security changed on September 11, 2001, and shattered the confidence of the nation's perception of invulnerability.

Homeland Security and Defense Post 9/11

At 8:46 am on September 11, 2001, American Airlines Flight 11, one of four hijacked airplanes in the sky that day, crashed into the North Tower of the World Trade Center (WTC). Exactly 15 minutes later, United Airlines Flight 175 hit the South Tower of the WTC. At 9:37 am, American Airlines Flight 77 struck the Pentagon. By 10:02 am, United Airlines Flight 93, the last hijacked plane, crashed into a field in Shanksville, PA, unable to reach its intended target

16

somewhere in Washington, DC.[47] In less than two hours, the four hijacked airliners had exacted a heavy toll in terms of loss of human life and infrastructure. The attacks further highlighted the shortfalls in the U.S. approach to homeland security and defense adopted by the nation since the end of the Cold War.

The immediate problem for national leaders on 9/11 was the security of U.S. airspace. This responsibility fell on the Federal Aviation Administration (FAA) working with the North American Aerospace Defense Command (NORAD).[48] At the time, the system for handling a hijacked airplane began with the air carrier contacting the FAA who in turn contacted NORAD for military support. However on 9/11, both the FAA and NORAD responded to a scenario they did not anticipate; a suicide hijacking originating from within the continental U.S.[49] Without clear protocols to handle such an event the National Command Authority "improvise[d] a homeland defense."[50]

The flawed focus of both the FAA and NORAD on 9/11 represented only one aspect of the homeland security and defense approach that failed to prevent the attacks. During the post-9/11 investigation, it became apparent to investigators that information regarding the terrorist plot existed prior to the event. For example, beginning in January 2000, the National Security Agency (NSA), CIA, and FBI began accumulating crucial information regarding the Al Qaeda hijackers.[51] In addition, by March 2001, multiple intelligence and law enforcement organizations, to include

---

[47]National Commission on Terrorist Attacks, *9/11 Commission Report* (New York: Barnes and Noble Publishing, 2004), 4-14. According to the report, investigators believe that terrorists aboard United Airlines Flight 93 intended to fly the aircraft into either The White House or the U.S. Capitol building.

[48] *9/11 Commission Report*, 14-17. The NORAD was established in 1958 between the U.S. and Canada for the collective defense of North American airspace.

[49] Ibid., 17-18.

[50] Ibid., 14.

[51] Ibid., 355-356.

17

the FBI and CIA, reported that an attack on U.S. soil was imminent.[52] However, in September 2001, these agencies were operating under an approach to national security geared to their specific agencies' requirements and not to a joint operating mindset.[53]

Because of the attacks on the Pentagon and WTC, the Bush Administration, undertook a massive restructuring of the organizational and operational approach to homeland security and defense. This restructuring included establishing the U.S. Northern Command, and Department of Homeland Security. The two organizations represent a concerted effort to integrate the elements of national power against future threats to the U.S. The overarching purpose of the new approach was to, "...streamline military assistance to civilian authorities ... [and inculcate national] preparedness and mitigation [of the threats to] the nation."[54] To date, these organizations serve as the foundation of the U.S. approach to homeland security and defense.

Threat Post-9/11

The events on 9/11 showed the government and the people of the United States that non-state actors possessed the capability to strike at strategic targets within the homeland. As stated in the 2001 *Quadrennial Defense Review*, "...the geographic position of the United States no longer guarantees immunity from direct attack on its population, territory, and infrastructure."[55] Since the attack, the threats of another 9/11 by groups such as Al Qaeda have become the primary focus of national security specialists and policy-makers. Even after nine years, scars of that day are still

---

[52] Ibid., 254-256.

[53] Ibid., 408.

[54] Lansford, Pauly, Jr., and Covarrubias, *To Protect and Defend: US Homeland Security Policy*, 84.

[55] U.S. Department of Defense, *Quadrennial Defense Review Report* (Washington, DC: Department of Defense September 30, 2001), 3, http://www.dod.gov/pubs/qdr2001.pdf (accessed February 11, 2012).

present in American society; as evinced by a 2010 poll indicating that U.S. households ranked terrorism as one of their top-three concerns for the nation. [56] However, post 9/11 threats to homeland security include more than just terrorism; it also includes the threat of widespread pandemic and natural disaster.

In the first decade of the 21st century, the threat of terrorism to homeland security arguably fell into three categories: Al Qaeda, Al Qaeda affiliates and allies, and homegrown terrorism. [57] These three categories serve as a framework to describe the terrorist threats to homeland security and help to explain Al Qaeda's direct and indirect influence, as well as external motivations on domestic terrorism. Between 2001 and 2010, the FBI documented twenty-seven cases that fit within the three terrorism categories mentioned above. Interestingly, Al Qaeda was directly responsible for only five of the twenty-seven plots. Affiliates accounted for three and most surprisingly homegrown violent extremists (HVE) accounted for sixteen incidents; roughly sixty-percent of the terrorist plots within the United States. [58]

The sixteen HVE terrorist plots account for the majority of terrorist activities within the U.S. from 2001 to 2010. Of these plots, six targeted the civilian population, five targeted the U.S. military, two targeted mass transit, one targeted the U.S. government, and two targeted a

---

[56] Pew Research Center, "Public's Priorities for 2010: Economy, Jobs, Terrorism," (Washington, DC: Pew Research Center for the People and the Press, January 25, 2010), 5, http://www.people-press.org/files/legacy-pdf/584.pdf (accessed February 11, 2012). In a poll taken by the Pew Research Center for the People and the Press, terrorism was in the top three concerns of group polled.

[57] Senate Committee on Homeland Security and Governmental Affairs, *Nine Years After 9/11: Confronting the Terrorist Threat to the Homeland,* 111th Cong., 2nd sess., 2010, http://www.hsgac.senate.gov/hearings/nine-years-after-9/11-confronting-the-terrorist-threat-to-the-homeland (accessed February 11, 2012).

[58] U.S. Department of Justice. *The Evolution of Terrorism Since 9/11*, by Lauren B. O'Brien. Washington, DC: Federal Bureau of Investigation, 2011, http://www fbi.gov/stats-services/publications /law-enforcement-bulletin/september-2011/the-evolution-of-terrorism-since-9-11 (accessed February 11, 2012).

combination of civilian population, U.S. government, financial, and aviation.[59] Although HVEs accounted for the majority of the terrorist plots within the U.S., only two of the sixteen were successful. One resulted in the death of a U.S. Soldier at a U.S. Army recruiting station in Little Rock, Arkansas, the other resulted in thirteen deaths at Fort Hood, Texas.[60]

The remaining terrorist plots recognized by the FBI from 2001 to 2010 came at the hands of either Al Qaeda or its affiliates. By the end of the decade, many intelligence analysts agreed that international counterterrorism efforts degraded Al Qaeda's ability to plan, resource, and conduct attacks, but its influence over other extremist groups and affiliates was on the rise.[61] These affiliates include the Yemen based Al Qaeda in the Arabian Peninsula (AQAP), and the Somalia based Al Shabaab.[62] These groups are responsible for facilitating terrorist plots within the U.S.; such as the failed 2009 bombing of a commuter jet over Detroit, and the failed 2010 air cargo bomb plot.[63]

In retrospect, there is no doubt that threats of terrorism within the homeland have dominated the post 9/11 environment. However, Hurricane Katrina and the H1N1 virus highlight the potential threats to homeland security caused by natural disasters and pandemics. Hurricane

---

[59] *The Evolution of Terrorism Since 9/11.*

[60] Jerome P. Bjelopera, *American Jihadist Terrorism: Combating a Complex Threat*, CRS Report for Congress R41416 (Washington, DC: Congressional Research Service, November 15, 2011), 92, 104, http://www.fas.org/sgp/crs/terror/R41416.pdf (accessed February 12, 2012).

[61] Daniel Benjamin, "Al Qaeda and Its Affiliates" (remarks, New America Foundation Conference, Washington, DC, April 27, 2011), http://www.state.gov/j/ct/rls/rm/2011/161895.htm (accessed February 13, 2012)

[62] John Rollins, *Al Qaeda and Affiliates: Historical Perspective, Global Presence, and Implications for U.S. Policy*, CRS Report for Congress R41070 (Washington, DC: Congressional Research Service, January 25, 2011), 14, 31, http://www.fas.org/sgp/crs/terror/R41070.pdf (accessed February 13, 2012).

[63] National Counterterrorism Center, Al Qaeda in the Arabian Peninsula (AQAP), Counterterrorism Calendar 2011, http://www.nctc.gov/site/groups/aqap html (accessed February 13, 2012); Rollins, *Al Qaeda and Affiliates: Historical Perspective, Global Presence, and Implications for U.S. Policy*, 16.

Katrina alone caused damage to over 90,000 square miles, killed over 1,300 people, and required a military response force of 70,000 active-duty and National Guardsmen.[64] Additionally, the 2009 H1N1 outbreak brought the sobering possibility of a highly contagious virus capable of causing over 2 million deaths in the U.S. alone.[65]

Terrorism, natural disaster, and pandemics highlight the major threats to homeland security in the first decade following the attacks on 9/11. Today, these threats remain. However, the upsurge in violence along the Southwest Border is quickly becoming just as dangerous, and could have far-reaching consequences.

Current Threat

Today, the instability along the nation's southwest border is potentially the most significant threat to homeland security the nation will face over the next decade. Although not fully realized because of the current homeland security focus on international terrorist organizations and weapons of mass destruction (WMD), DHS admits, "Transnational criminal organizations that have expanded efforts to cross our borders with illicit goods, currency, and trafficked persons represent a growing threat to the prosperity, security, and quality of life of U.S. citizens at home and abroad."[66] The DOD also shares the same developing concern.

On April 13, 2011, while addressing the Trilateral Seminar, Admiral (ADM) James A. Winnefield, former commander of NORTHCOM remarked, "As we [the U.S., Canada, Mexico]

---

[64] Government Accountability Office, *Hurricane Katrina: Better Plans and Exercises Needed to Guide the Military's Response to Catastrophic Natural Disasters* (Washington, DC: Government Accountability Office, 2006),10, 21, http://www.gao.gov/new.items/d06643.pdf (accessed February 13, 2012).

[65] Gail Brayman, "USNORTHCOM contributes pandemic flu contingency expertise to trilateral workshop," *northcom.mil/news*, April 14, 2008, http://www.northcom.mil/news/2008/041408.html (accessed February 14, 2012).

[66] *Quadrennial Homeland Security Review Report*, 2.

know, the TCOs are vicious in the extreme, better-armed than our police forces, very well-financed, diversified, and increasingly sophisticated in their methods. In fact, we now see TCOs using military equipment and tactics, including…submarines to move illegal drugs [into the U.S.].”[67] The evolving capability and sophistication of the TCOs underscore the emerging threat to U.S. national security. As outlined in the *Customs and Border Protection 2005 – 2010 Strategic Plan*, non-state actors such as Al Qaeda, “…continue to look for ways to circumvent U.S. security enhancements to strike Americans and the homeland… [and seek] to exploit the capabilities of established…smuggling networks, particularly on the Southwest Border.”[68] In a worst-case scenario, non-state actors leveraging the established TCO infiltration routes could possibly infiltrate and detonate a WMD within the homeland. However, understanding this worst-case scenario requires greater understanding of threat.

Numerous TCOs operate throughout the western hemisphere. The majority of the TCOs operating in the region either link directly to or support the ever-expanding global drug-trade. The support for the drug trade network spans from gangs to criminal states such as Venezuela.[69] This support, “…take[s] advantage of the legal, economic, and geographic interconnectedness of the hemisphere.”[70] To further their aims, criminal networks use the land, air, and sea domains to move goods, information, and personnel. With annual revenues in the billions of dollars, these

---

[67] http://www.northcom.mil/News/Transcripts/042011.html (accessed January 9, 2012).

[68] U.S. Department of Homeland Security, *Protecting America: U.S. Customs and Border Protection 2005-2010 Strategic Plan* (Washington, DC: Customs and Border Protection, May 2005), 9, http://www.aapa-ports.org/files/PDFs/CBP_5year_StrategicPlan.pdf (accessed March 22, 2012).

[69] Bob Killebrew and Jennifer Bernal, “Crime Wars: Gangs, Cartels and U.S. National Security,” Center for New American Security, September 2010, 13.

[70] Killebrew, Bernal, “Crime Wars: Gangs, Cartels and U.S. National Security,” 13.

organizations possess the means to continue their activities and the potential to outpace U.S. counter-efforts.

The Department of Justice's (DOJ) recently published, *National Drug Threat Assessment 2011*, highlights seven major trafficking organizations, based on their geographic origins that conduct operations into the United States: Mexican, Columbian, Ethnic Asian, Dominican, Cuban, and West African.[71] Although each organization plays a significant factor in illicit trafficking, the following threat analysis focuses on the major criminal organizations operating within Mexico. This is because, "Mexican-based TCOs and their associates dominate the supply and wholesale distribution of most illicit drugs in the United States."[72] Since 2007, the cartels operating within Mexico have waged an increasingly bloody war resulting in over 25,000 drug related deaths south of the border.[73]

Within Mexico, seven major TCOs dominate the illicit trafficking trade and smuggling routes into the United States. According to the DOJ, the seven leading Mexican-based TCO's are: Sinaloa Cartel, Los Zetas, Gulf Cartel, La Familia De Michoacan (LFM), Juarez Cartel, the Beltran Leyva Organization (BLO), and the Tijuana Cartel.[74] Each of these organizations competes with each other for control of the drug trade and routes leading into the United States. The violence along the southwest border is the byproduct of this competition.

---

[71] U.S. Department of Justice, *National Drug Threat Assessment 2011* (Washington, DC: National Drug Intelligence Center, 2011), 7-10, http://www.justice.gov/ndic/pubs44/44849/44849p.pdf (accessed January 22, 2012).

[72] *National Drug Threat Assessment 2011*, 7.

[73] Killebrew, Bernal, "Crime Wars: Gangs, Cartels and U.S. National Security," 15. This number was as of July 2010.

[74] *National Drug Threat Assessment 2011*, 7.

23

Of the seven cartels, the Sinaloa Cartel controls almost one-half of the drug trade in Mexico.[75] Led by Joaquin "El Chapo" Guzman, the cartel is organized into a federation of smaller organizations; making it difficult to dismantle. Controlling most of the west coast of Mexico, the Sinaloa Cartel mainly crosses into the U.S. through various entry points along the Arizona state border.

Although the Sinaloa Cartel is currently the largest cartel in Mexico, Los Zetas is arguably the most deadly. Founded by former special operations members from the Mexican military, the organization's inherent combat training and knowledge, "…allowed them to repeatedly outgun [Mexican] local and federal law enforcement officials."[76] Initially acting as guns-for-hire for the other Mexican-based cartels, "Los Zetas quickly established a reputation as one of the most violent enforcer gangs with military-level expertise in intelligence, weaponry, and operational tactics."[77] To put into context, the founding members of Los Zetas were, "reportedly trained at Fort Benning, Georgia, in special tactics, surveillance and countersurveillance, urban warfare, prison escape, hostage rescue, explosives use, and high-tech communications."[78] In 2009, Los Zetas took their knowledge and experience and formed their own drug trafficking cartel.[79] However, Dr. Max Manwaring, a Professor of Military Strategy in the Strategic Studies Institute of the U.S. Army War College, posits that Los Zetas ambitions do

[75] June S. Beittel, *Mexico's Drug Trafficking Organizations: Source and Scope of the Rising Violence*, CRS Report for Congress R41576 (Washington, DC: Congressional Research Service, January 7, 2011), 8, http://assets.opencrs.com/rpts/R41576_20110107.pdf (accessed January 22, 2012).

[76] Killebrew, Bernal, "Crime Wars: Gangs, Cartels and U.S. National Security," 21.

[77] June S. Beittel, *Mexico's Drug Related Violence*, CRS Report for Congress R40582 (Washington, DC: Congressional Research Service, May 27, 2009), 5, http://www.fas.org/sgp/crs/row/R40582.pdf (accessed January 22, 2012).

[78] Sylvia Longmire, "Mexican Drug War Contemporaries of Los Zetas," posted August 10, 2010, http://mexidata.info/id2361 html (accessed January 24, 2012).

[79] Beittel, *Mexico's Drug Trafficking Organizations: Source and Scope of the Rising Violence*, 10.

not stop at drug trafficking alone. He asserts that the organization,"… [aims to] expand operations into the territories of other cartels—and further challenge the sovereignty of the Mexican state."[80]

Perhaps the most unique approach by a cartel to win over the control of the populace and further their aims is La Familia. By infiltrating social, political, and religious organizations, the La Familia continues to increase their power-holdings over drug-trade and influence.[81] The cartel uses, "…religion…to portray the group's [LFM] assassinations of other cartel members and government officials as divine justice."[82] By using religion as a means to justify nefarious acts, the La Familia is similar to Islamist organizations such as Al Qaeda. Using this technique, the La Familia could pose a significant problem to both the Government of Mexico and U.S. homeland security.

Highlighted above are the cartels that pose the most immediate and potentially most significant threat to U.S. national security. Underscoring this assertion is President Barack Obama's 2009 designation of the Sinaloa, Los Zetas, and La Familia as Foreign Narcotics Kingpins which, "[D]eny significant foreign narcotics traffickers, their related businesses, and their operatives access to the U.S. financial system and to prohibit all trade and transactions between the traffickers and U.S. companies and individuals."[83] Concerning the Los Zetas specifically, in July 2011 President Obama issued an executive order which basically froze all property or assets belonging to the TCO because the organization, "…constitute[s] an unusual

---

[80] Max Manwaring, *A "New" Dynamic in the Western Hemisphere Security Environment: The Mexican Zetas and other Private Armies* (Carlisle, PA: Strategic Studies Institute, 2009), viii, http://www.strategicstudiesinstitute.army.mil/pdffiles/PUB940.pdf (accessed January 24, 2012).

[81] Killebrew, Bernal, "Crime Wars: Gangs, Cartels and U.S. National Security," 20-21.

[82] Ibid., 21.

[83] President, "Overview of the Foreign Narcotics Kingpin Designation Act," (Washington, DC: Office of the Press Secretary, April 15, 2009), http://www.whitehouse.gov/the_press_office/Fact-Sheet-Overview-of-the-Foreign-Narcotics-Kingpin-Designation-Act/ (accessed January 24, 2012).

and extraordinary threat to the national security, foreign policy, and economy of the United States."[84]

Although the Sinaloa, Los Zetas, and LFM currently dominate the illicit trafficking operations along the southwest border, the remaining four TCOs (Juarez Cartel, Tijuana Cartel, Gulf Cartel, and the BLO) continue to influence the operating environment, albeit on a lesser scale.[85] However, despite the ongoing power struggles between the cartels, all Mexican-based TCOs share a strategic aim to make profit.[86] Interestingly, this aim is manifesting itself as the U.S.-Mexican anti-drug efforts see more success. In many cases, the crackdowns on cross-border drug smuggling force the TCOs to look at different ways to turn a profit. In recent years, almost every cartel has branched out into other forms of crime to make up for lost revenue; including kidnapping and arms smuggling.[87] In addition, the increased security along the nation's border requires more elaborate and technologically advanced methods of moving goods.

As mentioned earlier, TCOs operating within Mexico harness all three domains (land, sea, and air) to move their products into and their money out of the United States. Some of these methods are simple, such as a vehicle or personnel carrying the product across the border. Some methods are so technologically advanced they conjure visions of nation-state think tanks with unlimited research and development budgets. Ultra-light aircraft, semi-submersible watercraft,

---

[84] Executive Order no. 13581, *Blocking Property of Transnational Criminal Organizations*, July 24, 2011, http://www.gpo.gov/fdsys/pkg/DCPD-201100523/pdf/DCPD-201100523.pdf (accessed January 25, 2012).

[85] Killebrew, Bernal, "Crime Wars: Gangs, Cartels and U.S. National Security," 20.

[86] Beittel, *Mexico's Drug Trafficking Organizations: Source and Scope of the Rising Violence*, 3.

[87] Manwaring, *A "New" Dynamic in the Western Hemisphere Security Environment: The Mexican Zetas and other Private Armies*, 18.

26

and tunneling all serve as examples of the more sophisticated methods currently used by TCOs.[88]

In addition, the TCOs have the latest in modern weaponry as evidenced by a recent report from

Reuters where a bag, believed to belong to a drug cartel , "[containing] a rocket launcher, grenade

launcher...and three packages of what appeared to be C-4 explosives," was discovered along the

Texas-Mexico border.[89]

The discourse over the ever-expanding and increasingly sophisticated scope and methods

of Mexican-based TCOs continues to gain momentum among homeland security strategists.

Many strategists blame the increasing violence along the southwest border to the U.S. drug-

abuser's unquenchable thirst for illicit narcotics. Remarks by Secretary Hillary Clinton in 2009

attest to this assertion when she stated, "...we [the U.S.] have accepted that this [fight against

TCOs] is a co-responsibility [between the U.S. and Mexico]. We know very well that the drug

traffickers are motivated by the demand for illegal drugs in the United States."[90] However, others

liken the events in Mexico to a "criminal insurgency."[91]

Army Field Manual (FM) 3-07, *Stability Operations*, defines insurgency as, "[a]n

organized movement aimed at the overthrow of a constituted government through use of

---

[88] U.S. Department of Homeland Security, "U.S. Border Patrol, Mexican Authorities Discover Two Tunnels," posted on January 12, 2012, http://www.cbp.gov/xp/cgov/newsroom/news_releases/ archives/2011_news_releases/january_2011/01122011_2.xml (accessed January 27, 2012). On January 9, 2011, CBP agents, along with Mexican authorities, discovered two uncompleted tunnels running between Mexico and the U.S. border. One tunnel was ten feet inside the United States.

[89] Jared Taylor, "U.S. Agents Find Rocket Launcher Near Mexico Border," *REUTERS.com*, September 14, 2011, http://www.reuters.com/article/2011/09/14/us-usa-mexico-weapons-idUSTRE78D7HK20110914?feedType=RSS&feedName=domesticNews (accessed January 27, 2012).

[90] Hillary Rodham-Clinton, "Remarks With Mexican Foreign Secretary Patricia Espinosa," (speech given at Mexico City, Mexico, March 25, 2009), http://www.state.gov/secretary /rm/ 2009a/03/120905.htm (accessed January 30, 2012).

[91] For a sampling of this literature, see John P. Sullivan and Adam Elkus, "Plazas for Profit: Mexico's Criminal Insurgency," *Small Wars Journal*, (April, 2009), http://smallwarsjournal.com/blog/ journal / docs-temp/232-sullivan.pdf?q=mag/docs-temp/232-sullivan.pdf (accessed January 27, 2012).

subversion and armed conflict."[92] However, FM 3-24, *Counterinsurgency*, also states, "an insurgency is an organized, protracted politico-military struggle designed to weaken the control and legitimacy of an established government, occupying power, or other political authority while increasing insurgent control."[93] Using this definition, Colonel (retired) Robert Killibrew asserts that TCOs operating within Mexico, "…are not simply a crime problem anymore, but a growing threat that is metastasizing into a new form of criminal insurgency."[94] Seen through this lens, the problem for U.S. law enforcement agencies becomes one of counterinsurgency; a problem that the U.S. Military has ten years of experience that would prove useful in the effort.

Future Threat

The fear of another spectacular attack by Al Qaeda still dominates the current and future threat environment. As U.S. and coalition efforts to defeat Osama Bin Laden's organization becomes more successful, Al Qaeda continues to shift its focus to training, resourcing, and inspiring affiliate groups to strike at the United States. Uncovered by U.S. law enforcement agencies, the disrupted plots of Al Qaeda and its affiliates evidence a combination of small and large-scale attacks. Despite this approach, Al Qaeda still seeks a large-scale attack within the United States. With the recent death of Osama Bin Laden, President Barack Obama asserts, "…al-Qa'Ida…will remain focused on striking the United States."[95] This assertion, coupled with

---

[92] U.S. Department of the Army, *Stability Operations,* FM 3-07 (Washington, DC: U.S. Department of the Army, October 2008), Glossary-6.

[93] U.S. Department of the Army, *Counterinsurgency,* FM 3-24 (Washington, DC: U.S. Department of the Army, December 2006), 1-1.

[94] Robert Killibrew, "Criminal Insurgency in the Americas and Beyond," *Prism* 2, no. 3 (June 2011), 34, http://www.ndu.edu/press/lib/images/prism2-3/Prism_33-52_Killebrew.pdf (accessed January 30, 2012)

[95] *National Strategy for Counterterrorism,* 3.

28

the increasing affiliation of extremist organizations and the means of infiltration provided by Mexican-based TCOs, provides a foundation for the future threat to U.S. homeland security.

In 2010, the U.S. Army published its future operating concept depicting the years 2016 to 2028. The concept, "…describes how future Army forces conduct operations as part of the joint force to deter conflict, prevail in war, and succeed in a wide range of contingencies in the future operational environment."[96] In their concept, the U.S. Army categorizes the future threat environment into a most likely and most dangerous scenario; the first being the continued threat of violent extremist groups and the second is a nation-state possessing WMDs intent on using it against targets within the United States. However, the U.S. Army concept also posits a third "dangerous alternative":

> Though neither most likely nor most dangerous, the threat of an individual or extremist organization employing a nuclear device in the U.S. is the most dangerous alternative. As worldwide proliferation of nuclear capabilities continues, adversarial regimes and extremist groups are likely to gain control of nuclear materials that, in turn, could be made available to rogue scientists. The U.S. has only a limited ability to detect and track nuclear components, and porous borders do little to prevent the movement of nuclear devices into or around the U.S. This limitation makes the U.S. vulnerable to such an attack.[97]

What makes this alternative scenario plausible is threefold: the results of successful U.S. and Mexican anti-narcotic efforts continue to force Mexican-based TCOs to seek out other forms of revenue (ends); extremist groups such as Al Qaeda continue to pursue attacks within the homeland and possess the monetary means and influence required to carry out their operations (ends and means); and Mexican-based TCO's have the capability to conduct illicit trafficking along the Southwest Border (ways).

---

[96] U.S. Department of the Army, *The United Stated Army Operating Concept 2016-2028*, TRADOC PAM 525-3-1 (Washington, DC: Department of the Army, August 19, 2010), iii, http://www.tradoc.army.mil/tpubs/pams/tp525-3-1.pdf (accessed February 18, 2012).

[97] *The United Stated Army Operating Concept 2016-2028*, 11.

Facilitating this future scenario is the continued deterioration of the Mexican

government's control over its territory. Since December 2006, when Mexican President Felipe

Calderon took office, drug related violence within Mexico claimed over 47,500 lives.[98] This is an

average of over 9,500 lives per year through the end of December 2011. Comparatively, this

number is on par with the number of American lives lost during the most difficult years of the

Vietnam War.[99] Although much of the loss of life directly attributes to competition amongst drug

cartels, it is a growing sign of the inability of the Mexican government to govern its people and

further weakens its credibility. This weakening of Mexican control over its territory has a direct

impact on the security of the homeland.

In 2008, Joint Forces Command (JFCOM) identified the collapse of the Mexican

government as one of two worst-case scenarios for the U.S Military. The former Functional

Combatant Command asserts, "[Mexico's] government, its politicians, police, and judicial

infrastructure are all under sustained assault and pressure by criminal gangs and drug

cartels…Any descent by Mexico into chaos would demand an American response based on the

serious implications for homeland security alone."[100] Two years later JFCOM assessed that for

the near future, "The Mexican government will remain severely challenged as its primary focus is

---

[98] British Broadcasting Corporation, "Q&A: Mexico's drug-related violence," *BBC.com,* January 25, 2012, http://www.bbc.co.uk/news/world-latin-america-10681249 (accessed February 18, 2012).

[99] U.S. National Archives, "Statistical information about casualties of the Vietnam War" http://www.archives.gov/research/military/vietnam-war/casualty-statistics html (accessed February 18, 2012). According to the National Archives, the average number of American deaths per year during the height of the Vietnam War (1965-1971) was 10,317 casualties/year.

[100] U.S. Department of Defense, *Joint Operating Environment*, (Washington, DC: Department of Defense, 2008), 36, http://www.jfcom.mil/newslink/storyarchive/2008/JOE2008.pdf (accessed February 15, 2012).

30

its fight against these formidable non-state groups [TCOs]."[101] Other high-ranking officials share this assessment. In a recent statement to a U.S. House of Representatives Homeland Security-related subcommittee, retired General and former Clinton Administration Drug Czar, Barry McCaffrey remarked, "Mexican drug trafficking organizations are active in Texas and their tentacles extend throughout the United States... we cannot allow local U.S. Sheriff's Departments and State Authorities along our two thousand mile border with Mexico to bear a disproportionate responsibility for defending America from large, violent, well-resourced criminal organizations."[102]

The rise in TCO-inspired violence within Mexico clearly trends toward a weakening of government control over Mexico. As highlighted above, this trend will continue into the near future. This trend undoubtedly results in degraded government control of the trafficking lines of operation between the U.S. and Mexico. In addition, the continued success of anti-narcotics operations by both the U.S. and international law enforcement agencies will force Mexican-based TCOs to seek alternate means of profit. The persistent aims of Al Qaeda and its affiliates, coupled with their ability to finance operations, represent not only a dangerous alternative, but also one that seems both most likely and most dangerous to U.S. national security.

---

[101] U.S. Department of Defense, *Joint Operating Environment*, (Washington, DC: Department of Defense, 2010), 48.

[102] Barry R. McCaffrey, "Statement for the Record Submitted by General Barry R. McCaffrey (USA, Ret)," (U.S. House of Representatives Committee on Homeland Security Subcommittee on Oversight, Investigations, and Management, Hearing on: "A Call to Action: Narco-Terrorism's Threat to the U.S. Southern Border"), 4, http://homeland.house.gov/sites/homeland house.gov/files/ Testimony%20McCaffrey.pdf (accessed February 15, 2012).

Response Post-9/11

USNORTHCOM became a combatant command in October 2002 after President Bush signed the updated Unified Command Plan.[103] Headquartered at Peterson Air Force Base, Colorado Springs, Colorado, NORTHCOM, "partners to conduct homeland defense, civil support, and security cooperation to defend and secure the United States and its interests."[104] Dual-hatted, the commander of NORTHCOM also commands NORAD. The command's area of responsibility extends 500 miles beyond the coast of the continental U.S. and includes Canada and Mexico.[105] Although the command has few assigned forces, eight subordinate headquarters provide coverage of the Combatant Command's area of responsibility in addition to NORAD. These headquarters include the Joint Task Force-Alaska (JTF-AK), Joint Task Force North (JTF-N), Joint Task Force Civil-Support (JTF-CS), Joint Force Headquarters National Capital Region (JFHQ-NCR), Army North, Air Force North, U.S. Fleet Forces Command, and U.S. Marine Forces Northern Command.[106] In addition, "The Northern Command is also charged with coordinating the [USNG] response to domestic events and, where Guard units are serving in federal homeland capacity, commanding those units."[107]

Despite the support of the entire U.S. military behind it, NORTHCOM must operate within the U.S. legal framework. The Posse Comitatus Act prevents the military from participating in law enforcement without direct approval by the Secretary of Defense or President.

---

[103] United States Northern Command, About USNORTHCOM, http://www.northcom.mil/About/index.html (accessed February 6, 2012).

[104] Ibid.

[105] Ibid.

[106] Ibid.

[107] James E. Baker, *In the Common Defense: National Security Law for Perilous Times* (New York: Cambridge University Press, 2007), 266.

32

Originally created in response to allegations that the U.S. military influenced voters during the 1876 Presidential election, the Posse Comitatus Act and military directives explicitly prohibit federal troops from providing direct assistance to law enforcement organizations that include interdiction, search and seizure, arrest, and surveillance.[108] However, the Posse Comitatus Act does not apply to USNG personnel when not in federal service.

Although active-duty U.S. military personnel cannot directly assist law enforcement organizations, exceptions to the law exist. The Posse Comitatus Act precludes active assistance; however, the active-duty military can provide assistance through passive assistance. Passive assistance to law enforcement agencies include loaning of equipment, sharing of intelligence, and providing training.[109]

The military refers to this passive assistance as civil support operations. Joint U.S. military doctrine subdivides civil support operations into three categories: domestic emergencies, designated law enforcement support, and other activities.[110] An example of passive assistance to civil authorities is the *Chairman of the Joint Chiefs of Staff Instruction* (CJCSI) *3710.10B* which provides, "...authority and guidance to CDRUSSOUTHCOM [Commander, U.S. Southern Command] for domestic CD [counterdrug]/law enforcement activities... [and] promulgates SecDef [Secretary of Defense] authority to Military Department Secretaries to relinquish forces to CDRUSNORTHCOM [Commander, U.S. Northern Command] to exercise TACON [tactical

---

[108] Baker, *In the Common Defense: National Security Law for Perilous Times*, 268-269.

[109] Lansford, Pauly, Jr., and Covarrubias, *To Protect and Defend: US Homeland Security Policy*, 93.

[110] U.S. Department of Defense, *Civil Support,* JP 3-28 (Washington, DC: Department of Defense, September 14, 2007), III-1.

control] to conduct CD operational support to US LEAs [law enforcement agencies]."[111]

Although the directive allows for U.S. military assets domestically, the request for support must come from a local, state, or federal law enforcement agency and receive approval by the Secretary of Defense.

Besides support to law enforcement agencies, the U.S. military may play a significant role in homeland security during domestic emergencies.[112] Federal law allows for the use of the military in support of civil authorities through the *Robert T. Stafford Disaster Relief and Emergency Assistant Act* (Stafford Act). Found in United States Code (USC) 42, The Public Health, and Welfare, the Stafford Act states:

> During the immediate aftermath of an incident which may ultimately qualify for assistance…the Governor of the State in which such incident occurred may request the President to direct the Secretary of Defense to utilize the resources of the Department of Defense for the purpose of performing on public and private lands any emergency work which is made necessary by such incident and which is essential for the preservation of life and property. If the President determines that such work is essential for the preservation of life and property, the President shall grant such request to the extent the President determines practicable.[113]

Although available to state governors, the Stafford Act typically applies only in cases where an emergency far exceeds the resources of local, state, and federal civilian organizations.

---

[111] U.S. Department of Defense, *DOD Counterdrug Support*, CJCSI 3710.10B, January 26, 2007, 1-2, http://www.dtic.mil/cjcs_directives/cdata/unlimit/3710_01.pdf (accessed December 28, 2011). This directive allows for U.S. military assistance in: aerial and ground reconnaissance, tunnel detection support, diver support, linguist and intelligence analyst support, transportation support, equipment and operations support, C4I (command, control, communications, computer, and intelligence) support, and technology demonstrations.

[112] *Civil Support*, GL-7. Joint doctrine defines domestic emergencies as, "Emergencies affecting the public welfare and occurring within the 50 states, District of Columbia, Commonwealth of Puerto Rico, US possessions and territories, or any political subdivision thereof, as a result of enemy attack, insurrection, civil disturbance, earthquake, fire, flood, or other public disasters or equivalent emergencies that endanger life and property or disrupt the usual process of government. Domestic emergencies include civil defense emergencies, civil disturbances, major disasters, and natural disasters."

[113] Department of Homeland Security, *Robert T. Stafford Disaster Relief and Emergency Assistance Act, as Amended, and Related Authorities*, (Washington, DC: Federal Emergency Management Agency, June 2007), i, 28, http://www.fema.gov/pdf/about/stafford_act.pdf (accessed December 30, 2011).

Additionally, DOD forces act in support of civil authorities, because within U.S. borders, executive civilian agencies such as the DHS serve as the lead federal agency.[114]

On November 22, 2002, President George W. Bush signed the Homeland Security Act of 2002 and with it created the DHS. During the signing of the Act, President Bush stated, "The new Department [DHS] will analyze threats, will guard our borders and airports, protect critical infrastructure, and coordinate the response of our Nation to future emergencies."[115] Three pivotal events serve as touch-points that mark the evolution of the DHS since its inception. The first of these events is its creation in 2002, followed by the reforms following Hurricane Katrina, and finally the publishing of the 2010 *Quadrennial Homeland Security Review*.[116] Each of these events resulted in policy and organizational changes that follow realized threats to homeland security.

In March 2003, the DHS became an independent "cabinet-level department to further coordinate and unify national homeland security efforts."[117] At the outset, the DHS was comprised of 22 agencies to include the U.S. Coast Guard (USCG), CBP, and the Federal Emergency Management Agency (FEMA). The department divided itself into four directorates: Border and Transportation Security, Emergency Preparedness and Response, Science and

---

[114] Louise Stanton, *The Civilian-Military Divide: Obstacles to the Integration of Intelligence in the United States* (Santa Barbara, CA: Praeger Security International, 2009), 58-59, 61-62. Rarely implemented, two additional authorities exist that authorize U.S. military support: a request by state governors in cases of insurrection, and the unilateral Presidential authority to employ active-duty and National Guard troops in cases of rebellion (10 USC 331,332,333).

[115] Maxwell, *Homeland Security: A Documentary History*, 432.

[116] *Quadrennial Homeland Security Review Report*, iii.

[117] U.S. Department of Homeland Security, Creation of the Department of Homeland Security, http://www.dhs.gov/xabout/history/gc_1297963906741.shtm.

Technology, and Information Analysis and Infrastructure.[118] As the newest member in the cabinet, the DHS initially focused its full weight on preparing for and preventing terrorist attacks against the U.S.; not knowing what other threats to homeland security were lurking around the corner.[119]

On August 29, 2005, just a month after the DHS Second Stage Review, a category five hurricane named Katrina, smashed into the Gulf States of Louisiana and Mississippi.[120] In its wake, the hurricane caused billions of dollars in damage, over 1,300 deaths, left more than a million people without homes, and highlighted how unprepared federal and state emergency responders were in dealing with catastrophic natural disasters.[121] For example, in the immediate aftermath of the hurricane, Wal-Mart replaced FEMA as the main supplier of essential supplies into the New Orleans region.[122] Because of the inadequate response to the massive hurricane, President Bush signed the Post-Katrina Emergency Reform Act in October 2006, which consolidated a broader spectrum of disaster relief functions under FEMA.

The last major point in the evolution of DHS was the release of the *Quadrennial Homeland Security Review*. The review offers, "… [a] strategic framework to guide the activities of participants in homeland security toward a common end."[123] Representing just over seven years of maturation, the document clearly delineates the department's five core missions, and

---

[118] Lansford, Pauly, Jr., and Covarrubias, *To Protect and Defend: US Homeland Security Policy*, 85.

[119] Christopher Cooper and Robert Block, *Disaster: Hurricane Katrina and the Failure of Homeland Security* (New York: Henry Holt and Company, 2006), xiii.

[120] U.S. Department of Homeland Security, Creation of the Department of Homeland Security. Occurring in July 2005, the DHS Second Stage Review resulted in a "six-point agenda" that realigned the structure of the department.

[121] Cooper, Block, *Disaster: Hurricane Katrina and the Failure of Homeland Security*, 223-226.

[122] Ibid., 262-264.

[123] *Quadrennial Homeland Security Review Report*, iii.

provides goals and objectives for those missions.[124] In addition, this document provides a set of

strategic aims and subsequent objectives for improving the U.S. homeland security approach. One

of these strategic aims, Foster Unity of Effort, expressly states the necessity of partnering with the

DOD to enhance DHS capability. This strategic objective seeks to develop ways to, "jointly

develop capabilities necessary for both defense and homeland security."[125] This strategic

objective acknowledges that to deter, prevent, and defeat current threats takes the combined

efforts of both the U.S. military and civilian agencies.

The events on 9/11 proved that proved that small and seemingly inconsequential groups

had the capability to plan and carry out attacks in the homeland. To determine how the terrorists

were able to accomplish their mission and to prevent another attack on U.S. soil, "…Congress

and the President created the National Commission on Terrorist Attacks Upon the United States

(Public Law 107-306, November 27, 2002)."[126] The report flatly states that the "The nation was

unprepared" and highlighted the need for major changes in the national approach to domestic

security.[127]

This new approach, highlighted by the creation of NORTHCOM and DHS, represents the

largest reorganization of the federal government since the National Security Act of 1947.[128] The

reorganization was necessary due to the failure of the homeland security approach adopted after

the Cold War. The two organizations seek to provide a layered homeland defense with the U.S.

---

[124] Ibid, x.

[125] *Quadrennial Homeland Security Review Report*, 71-74.

[126] National Commission on Terrorist Attacks, *9/11 Commission Report* (New York: Barnes and Noble Publishing, 2004), xv.

[127] National Commission on Terrorist Attacks, *9/11 Commission Report* (New York: Barnes and Noble Publishing, 2004), xv.

[128] Lansford, Pauly, Jr., and Covarrubias, *To Protect and Defend: US Homeland Security Policy*, 85.

37

military focusing outside the nation's borders, civilian agencies focusing inside, and

NORTHCOM and DHS ensure bridging the two layers. Both organizations continue to evolve to

the changing conditions as highlighted by the DHS *Quadrennial Homeland Security Review*.[129]

Homeland Security and Defense Today

Currently NORTHCOM is involved in a number of joint military and interagency

activities throughout its area of operations. These activities include air defense of the nation's

capital, providing support to law enforcement agencies along the northern and southern U.S.

border, theater security cooperation with Canada and Mexico, and missile defense. In addition to

these enduring missions, during the summer of 2011 NORTHCOM also provided military planes

to suppress wildfires in both Texas and the Northwest, and rotary-wing aircraft to assist in

recovery efforts during Hurricane Irene. Although only a snapshot of the myriad of efforts

ongoing within the command, the numerous civil-support, and homeland defense activities

highlight the diverse nature of NORTHCOMs mission.

The diversity in NORTHCOM mission sets is crucial to U.S. national security. However,

for the purposes of this analysis, the remainder of the discussion will focus on the command's

support to the CBP and ICE. This support, provided by JTF-North, currently falls into six general

categories: operational support, intelligence support, engineering support, general support,

interagency synchronization, and technology integration.[130]

Originally called Joint Task Force-6, JTF-North gained its new designation in 2004 and

assumed its current mission; "support[ing] Drug Law Enforcement Agencies in the conduct of

---

[129] *Quadrennial Homeland Security Review Report*, 36.

[130] Joint Task Force North, Homeland Security Support, http://www.jtfn.northcom.mil/subpages/
homeland_s.html (accessed February 21, 2012).

Counter Drug/Counter Narco-Terrorism operations in the NORTHCOM area of responsibility to disrupt trans-national criminal organizations and deter their freedom of action in order to protect the homeland."[131] From 2010 to 2012, JTF-North executed its mission by supporting law enforcement agencies operating on the Southwest Border through road improvement, barrier emplacement, ground sensor emplacement, and assisting CBP with intelligence gathering on border penetrations.[132]

Capabilities Assessment

The description of the operational environment, outlined in the previous chapters, highlight the evolutionary threat-response framework of the U.S. Military and law enforcement in regards to homeland defense and security. Each threat, whether it came in the form of an internal threat such as the Klu Klux Klan, or an external threat such as Al Qaeda, elicited a response by the organizations responsible for the safeguarding of the nation. Most often, these changes in the operational environment went unwarranted until it resulted in a catastrophic event; such as the attacks on 9/11. However, mistakes do not need to repeat themselves.

Many indicators show that the future threat to national security leads to what the U.S. Army posits as a "dangerous alternative". The combination of the ends and means of extremist groups, such as AQAP, coupled with the ways provided by Mexican-based TCOs, makes the

---

[131] Joint Task Force North, Joint Task Force North Mission, http://www.jtfn northcom mil/ subpages/mission.html (accessed February 21, 2012); Joint Task Force North, "Fact Sheet: Joint Task Force North, " Fact Sheet #2, January 11, 2011, http://www.jtfn.northcom.mil/factsheets/ 2_11jan11history.pdf (accessed February 21, 2012).

[132] Joint Task Force North, "Fact Sheet: Joint Task Force North, " Fact Sheet #5, January 11, 2011, http://www.jtfn northcom mil/factsheets/5_11jan11eng_sppt.pdf (accessed February 21, 2012); Armando Carrasco, "2nd Intel Battalion Supports Border Patrol in South Texas," May 2, 2011, http://www.marines mil/unit/iimef/Pages/2ndIntelBorderPatrol.aspx (accessed February 21, 2012); Mark Rockwell, "JTF North to aid CBP in NM and AZ in February," *GSNmagazine.com*, February 10, 2012, http://www.gsnmagazine.com/node/25619 (accessed February 21, 2012).

39

dangerous alternative a more realistic future. Preventing this combination of ends, ways, and means is the problem; not only for the U.S. military, but also for law enforcement agencies. So the question becomes; how to prevent this scenario from becoming reality?

The CBP and ICE stand ready as the front-line defense against this emerging threat, but some critics oppose this approach, and prefer the U.S. military assume responsibility for border security.[133] However, the issue is not as black and white as what the critics may argue. True, the U.S. military has ten years fighting an insurgency in Iraq and Afghanistan, but also true is federal laws prevent such an act and CBP and ICE have proven themselves as effective organizations capable of protecting the nation's borders. This said, the ideal solution is one where the U.S. military leverages, "… lessons learned from ten years of countering a different irregular threat overseas," to assist the CBP and ICE in their efforts.[134]

Current NORTHCOM Capabilities

As mentioned earlier, NORTHCOM currently has eight subordinate commands to conduct its homeland defense and Defense Support of Civil Authorities (DSCA) operations. However, four of the commands (Army North, Air Force North, U.S. Fleet Forces Command, and U.S. Marine Forces Northern Command), serve as service component headquarters.[135] Each of

---

[133] Dave Gibson, "The U.S. Military should be used to defend our border with Mexico," *Examiner.com*, January, 28, 2010, http://www.examiner.com/immigration-reform-in-national/the-u-s-military-should-be-used-to-defend-our-border-with-mexico#ixzz1n4k6EF91 (accessed February 21, 2012).

[134] James A. Winnefeld, "Statement before the House Armed Services Committee," March 30, 2011, 7, http://www.northcom.mil/Docs/2011%20NORAD%20and%20USNORTHCOM%20 Posture% 20Statement %20(HASC%20Final).pdf (accessed February 21, 2012).

[135] U.S. Department of Defense, *Doctrine for the Armed Forces of the United States*, JP-1 (Washington, DC: Department of Defense, May 2, 2007), GL-9. According to Joint doctrine, a service component command is, "A command consisting of the Service component commander and all those Service forces, such as individuals, units, detachments, organizations, and installations under that

the service component commands possesses the capability to command and control their unique service's capabilities in the event of a DSCA operation. Despite this crucial capability, each service component command has very few assigned forces and therefore few capabilities as they apply to assisting efforts on the Southwest border.[136]

The remaining four subordinate commands (JTF-North, JTF-Alaska, JTF-CS, and JFHQ-NCR), have very few assigned forces, and therefore very few capabilities, as well. All of the Joint commands possess the capability to command and control forces when assigned by the Secretary of Defense or President. However, JTF-Alaska and JFHQ-NCR focus their capabilities in Alaska and the National Capital Region respectfully, and any capability they possess cannot apply to efforts on the Southwest Border. This leaves only JTF-North and JTF-CS as the two subordinate headquarters to assess current capabilities as they apply to this analysis.

Joint Task Force-North's current capabilities reside in its multi-faceted command and control, planning capacity, authority to assist law enforcement agencies in counterdrug operation, and access to the global pool of military capabilities within DOD.[137] Joint Task Force-Civil Support's current capabilities reside in its ability to respond to a chemical, biological, radiation, and nuclear (CBRN) incident. It does this through its CBRN response force (CBRN); manned by over 5,000 personnel and organized into two subordinate force packages. The JTF-CS CBRN is

---

command, including the support forces that have been assigned to a combatant command or further assigned to a subordinate unified command or joint task force."

[136] For more information on NORTHCOM's service component commands, visit www.northcom.mil.

[137] Joint Task Force North, Joint Task Force North Overview, http://www.jtfn.northcom mil/ factsheets/jtfnorth_command_brief_mar2010.pdf (accessed February 25, 2012).

capable of providing decontamination, search and rescue, engineer support, security, medical support, aviation support, and logistic capabilities.[138]

Current CBP Capabilities

The mission of CBP is to, "… [Keep] terrorists and their weapons out of the U.S. It also has a responsibility for securing and facilitating trade and travel while enforcing hundreds of U.S. regulations, including immigration and drug laws."[139] To do this, the organization employs over 21,000 border patrol agents and boasts having, "… the world's largest aviation and maritime law enforcement organization."[140] In addition, to these capabilities, CBP also employs a wide range of technologically advanced sensors and communications equipment. In total, over 85 percent of CBP border officers and their equipment currently operate along the Southwest Border.[141]

Unlike the doctrine-based U.S. military, the CBP governs its operations through strategic and regulatory guidance. For example, the *CPB Strategic Plan 2009-2014* provides the goals and objectives for the organization in an attempt to unify organizational efforts.[142] Underlying this overarching guidance are specific instructions to the national and international community for the entrance of personnel and goods into the United States. Referred to as publications, these

---

[138] Joint Task Force Civil Support, JTF-CS 101 Brief, http://www.jtfn.northcom.mil/factsheets /jtfnorth_command_brief_mar2010.pdf (accessed February 25, 2012).

[139] U.S. Customs and Border Protection, *About CBP*, http://www.cbp.gov/xp/cgov/about/ (accessed March 11, 2012).

[140] U.S. Department of Homeland Security, "Snapshot: A Summary of CBP facts and figures" (Washington, DC: U.S. Customs and Border Protection, February 2012), http://www.cbp.gov/linkhandler/ cgov/about/accomplish/cbp_snapshot.ctt/snapshot.pdf (accessed March 12, 2012).

[141] Chad C. Haddal, *Border Security: The Role of the U.S. Border Patrol*, CRS Report for Congress RL32562 (Washington, DC: Congressional Research Service, August 11, 2010), 7, 13, http://www.fas.org/sgp/crs/homesec/RL32562.pdf (accessed March 12, 2012).

[142] U.S. Department of Homeland Security, *Secure Border, Safe Travel, Legal Trade: U.S. Customs and Border Protection Fiscal Year 2009-2014 Strategic Plan* (Washington, DC: Customs and Border Protection, July 2009), 13-20.

42

directives inform personnel entering and exiting the U.S. on regulations ranging from international travel to exporting an automobile. In addition, these guidelines provide Border Enforcement Agents the authority within which they carry out their border interdiction duties.[143]

To carry out these duties, the CBP organizes itself along the Southwest Border in nine sectors. From west to east, these sectors are San Diego, El Centro, Yuma, Tucson, El Paso, Big Bend, Del Rio, Laredo, and Rio Grande Valley.[144] Within each zone, the CBP manages its assigned areas through smaller stations. Across the nine zones, there are seventy-three stations.[145] Manning these stations stands the border patrol officer. The backbone of the CBP, the border patrol officer is responsible for carrying out the day-to-day enforcement of protecting the nation's border. However, when incidents occur requiring a more specialized capability, such as reconnaissance and surveillance or search and rescue, the CBP calls on the Border Patrol Special Operations Group (BORSOG). Mirrored on the model of U.S. military special operations, the BORSOG consists of Border Patrol Tactical Unit (BORTAC); Border Patrol Search, Trauma, and Rescue (BORSTAR); and at the sector level, Border Patrol Special Response Team (BORSRT).[146]

Supporting the ground operations along the Southwest Border is a unique organization within CBP known as the Office of Air and Marine (OAM). Comprised of 270 aircraft and 280

---

[143] U.S. Customs and Border Protection, *CBP Newsroom*, http://www.cbp.gov/xp/cgov/newsroom/ publications/ (accessed April 10, 2012).

[144] National Immigration Forum, "Backgrounder: Southwest Border Security Operations" (Washington, DC: National Immigration Forum, December 2010), 1, http://www.immigrationforum.org/ images/uploads/SouthwestBorderSecurityOperations.pdf (accessed March 12, 2012).

[145] U.S. Customs and Border Protection, Border Patrol Sectors, http://www.cbp.gov/xp/cgov/ border_security/border_patrol/border_patrol_sectors/ (accessed March 12, 2012).

[146] U.S. Customs and Border Protection, "Fact Sheet: Border Patrol Special Operations Group" http://www.cbp.gov/linkhandler/cgov/newsroom/fact_sheets/border/border_patrol/bp_sog.ctt/bp_sog.pdf (accessed March 12, 2012).

watercraft, the OAM provides the CBP with the capability to, "… detect, interdict, and prevent acts of terrorism and the unlawful movement of people, illegal drugs and other contraband toward or across U.S. borders."[147] In the air, the OAM accomplishes this with platforms such as the UH-60 Blackhawk helicopter, P-3 Orion fixed winged aircraft, and the MQ-9 Predator unmanned aerial system (UAS). These aircraft have the latest in sensor technology including radar and infrared optics.[148] On the water, OAM has six variants, ranging from small to medium sized boats, capable of interdiction operations in coastal waters. These craft have long-range communication, radar, forward-looking infrared, and weapon mounts for medium machine guns.[149]

To meet strategic goals, validate the current organizational construct, and ensure proper employment of the agencies assets, CBP possesses multiple training centers. For example, the CBP maintains the U.S. Customs and Border Protection National Air Training Center in Oklahoma, where the organization assesses and trains future pilots, "… on interdiction, use of night vision goggles (NVGs) and other law-enforcement-specific areas."[150] In addition, CBP also maintains the Border Patrol Academy in New Mexico. This institution teaches newly recruited

---

[147] U.S. Customs and Border Protection, "Fact Sheet: Office of Air and Marine" http://www.cbp.gov/linkhandler/cgov/newsroom/fact_sheets/marine/air_marine.ctt/air_marine.pdf (accessed March 12, 2012).

[148] U.S. Customs and Border Protection, Aviation Asset Slicks, http://www.cbp.gov/xp/cgov/border_security/air_marine/air/aviation_asset/ (accessed March 12, 2012).

[149] U.S. Customs and Border Protection, Marine Asset Slicks, http://www.cbp.gov/xp/cgov/border_security/ air_marine/marine/marine_asset/ (accessed March 12, 2012).

[150] Brent Holman, "US Customs and Border Protection widens air role," *Professional Pilot Magazine,* February 2009, http://www.propilotmag.com/archives/2009/Feb09/A2_USCustoms_p1.html (accessed April 10, 2012).

Border Patrol Agents in subjects ranging from integrated law and marksmanship to language proficiency.[151] However, the majority of training within CBP focuses on entry-level recruits.

Current ICE Capabilities

The mission of ICE is to, "… [P]romote homeland security and public safety through the criminal and civil enforcement of federal laws governing border control, customs, trade, and immigration."[152] Unlike the CBP, which focuses on physically securing the nation's border, ICE serves as the, "… principle investigative arm of the U.S. Department of Homeland Security."[153] Like the CBP, ICE lacks the DOD's detailed doctrine to guide operations. However, since the agency focuses on investigation, ICE operates within the legal authorities given to it by Congress.

Despite the impressive arsenal of border security officers, aircraft, watercraft, and sensors organized under the CBP, ICE possesses legal authorities that allow its organization to look beyond the U.S.-Mexican border. For example, ICE has the authorities,"… granted under Title 18—General Smuggling, Title 19—Customs Duties and Title 21—Narcotics Violations to investigate the full spectrum of smuggling crimes."[154] These authorities are crucial to the overall effort along the Southwest Border, because they provide ICE with the means to investigate TCO operations at its source. For this reason, ICE is not only the investigative arm of DHS, but also

---

[151] U.S. Customs and Border Protection, *Border Patrol Academy*, http://borderpatrolacademy.com/ (accessed April 10, 2012).

[152] U.S. Immigration and Customs Enforcement, About ICE: Overview, http://www.ice.gov/about/ overview/ (accessed March 11, 2012).

[153] Ibid.

[154] U.S. Department of Homeland Security, *ICE Investigations: Mission Roles in Multi-Agency Areas of Responsibility* (Washington, DC: Immigration and Customs Enforcement, August 2007), 2, http://www.fbiic.gov/public/2008/may/ICE_Mission_Roles.pdf (accessed March 13, 2012).

serves as the, "… primary investigative arm for CBP Field Operations."[155] Although this title

conjures visions of seamless cooperation, existing collaborative challenges between the two

organizations still exist.

Organizationally, ICE accomplishes its mission on the Southwest Border through its

Border Enforcement Task Force. These multi-agency organizations, "… focus their investigative

efforts on alien smuggling, drug smuggling, firearms smuggling, and transnational gangs."[156] Of

the twenty-two Border Enforcement Task Force Teams organized, nine operate along the

Southwest Border.[157] The teams integrate with other interagency and international partners

including CBP and Mexico to accomplish its mission. Many, including current DHS Secretary

Janet Napolitano, see the Border Enforcement Task Force as a bridge to the not only the gap in

interagency cooperation, but also a bridge between U.S. and Mexico cross-border investigative

relations.[158]

To effectively harness the investigative capabilities of ICE and ensure its continued

success, the organization has the Office of Training and Development. Responsible for technical,

educational, and career programs, the directorate ensures the agency utilizes its limited resources

[155] U.S. Department of Homeland Security, *DHS' Progress In Addressing Coordination Challenges Between Customs and Border Protection and Immigration and Customs Enforcement* (Washington, DC: Office of Inspector General, April 2007), 8, http://www.oig.dhs.gov/assets/Mgmt /OIG_07-38_Apr07.pdf (accessed March 14, 2012).

[156] *ICE Investigations: Mission Roles in Multi-Agency Areas of Responsibility*, 4. BEST teams incorporate personnel from ICE; U.S. Customs and Border Protection (CBP); Drug Enforcement Administration (DEA); Bureau of Alcohol, Tobacco, Firearms and Explosives; Federal Bureau of Investigation; U.S. Coast Guard; and the U.S. Attorney's Office along with other key federal, state, local and foreign law enforcement agencies

[157] U.S. Immigration and Customs Enforcement, "Fact Sheet: Border Enforcement Security Task Force (BEST)," http://www.ice.gov/news/library/factsheets/best htm (accessed March 13, 2012).

[158] House Committee on Homeland Security, *U.S. Homeland Security Role in the Mexican War Against Drug Cartels*, 112th Cong., 1st sess., March 31, 2012, 5, http://www.hsdl.org/?view&did=7774 (accessed April 11, 2012).

more effectively.[159] This training, focused on the new recruit, focuses on surveillance, marksmanship, and physical fitness. [160] However, beyond this initial training ICE possesses few programs for advanced training and education.

Required Capabilities

To combat a likely alliance between the Mexican-based TCOs and extremist groups, CBP and ICE require effective capabilities to interdict illicit smuggling across the Southwest Border. Joint U.S. Doctrine defines interdiction as, "… activities conducted to divert, disrupt, delay, intercept, board, detain, or destroy, as appropriate, vessels, vehicles, aircraft, people, and cargo."[161] Despite this definition, current military doctrine lacks detailed requirements for units (or organizations) involved in border interdiction. However, Vietnam era U.S. military doctrine provides a framework for border interdiction and the necessary capabilities required for mission accomplishment.

According to FM 31-55 *Border Security / Anti-infiltration Operations*, which was written during the Vietnam War, the required capabilities for successful border security and interdiction are: detection; command, control, and communications; response forces; air surveillance; and electronic warfare.[162] Although this doctrine is more than forty years old, the

---

[159] U.S. Immigration and Customs Enforcement, "Office of Training & Development (OTD)," http://www.ice.gov/about/offices/management-administration/otd/ (accessed April 11, 2012).

[160] U.S. Department of Homeland Security, *Surveillance Lesson Plan Field Operations Training Plan* (Washington, DC: Immigration and Customs Enforcement, February 2011), 5, www.michiganimmigrant.org/advocate_library/ice_training.../file (accessed April 11, 2012);

[161] *Department of Defense Dictionary of Military and Associated Terms*, 239.

[162] U.S. Department of the Army, *Border Security/ Anti-Infiltration Operations,* FM 31-55 (Washington, DC: Department of the Army, 1968), 1-5 to 1-6, http://www.ebookdb.org/reading /G216621AG67348743A2B7F69/Border-Securityanti-infiltration-Operations (accessed February 26, 2012).

47

identified capabilities still hold true today. For example, the most recent CBP strategic plan identifies five strategic objectives that directly nest with the 1968 U.S. Army doctrine for border security.[163] For the most part, CBP and ICE possess the material capabilities required for border interdiction and security. So why do these agencies only interdict ten percent of illicit trafficking?

The required capabilities to effectively safeguard the nation's border and prevent the realization of the "dangerous alternative" require a comprehensive approach involving JTF-North, CBP, and ICE. This comprehensive approach requires unity of effort, intelligence sharing, air and maritime coordination, and cooperative strategic planning between ICE and CBP. In addition, JTF-North requires the authority, capability, and manpower to assist its interagency partners along the Southwest Border.

These required capabilities ensure that the CBP and ICE have the capacity and support to meet the emerging threat posed by extremist groups and TCOs along the Southwest Border. Although based on former U.S. Army doctrine, the capabilities nest with the first strategic goal, "Secure the Nation's borders to protect America from the entry of dangerous people and goods and prevent unlawful trade and travel," outlined in the CBP strategic plan.[164] Additionally, the required capabilities nest with ICE strategic objective 3.2, which the agency seeks to, "…strengthen relationships and collaboration with CBP."[165] However, current JTF-North, CBP, and

---

[163] *Secure Border, Safe Travel, Legal Trade: U.S. Customs and Border Protection Fiscal Year 2009-2014 Strategic Plan*, 11-12. According to the CBP strategic plan: Goal 1.2 and 1.3 nest with detection; *Cross-Cutting Enablers* nests with C3 and EW; Goal 1.1 nests with air surveillance; and Goal 1.4 nests with response.

[164] Ibid., 11.

[165] U.S. Department of Homeland Security, *U.S. Immigration and Customs Enforcement Strategic Plan FY 2010-2014* (Washington, DC: Immigration and Customs Enforcement, June 2010), 5, http://www.ice.gov/about/overview/ (accessed March 15, 2012).

ICE capabilities do not meet the requirements for a comprehensive approach for effective border interdiction operations.

Capability Gaps

The current gaps in capability necessary for effective border interdiction operations prevent a more holistic approach to combat the emerging threats posed by Mexican-based TCOs and extremist groups. These gaps fall into two categories: gaps in capability between CBP and ICE; and gaps in capability of JTF-North to support the interagency in their operations. Within the first category, ICE and CBP lack unity of effort, effective intelligence fusion, air cooperation and coordination, and the capacity to operationally control the entire Southwest Border. Within the second category, JTF-North lacks authority, military capability, manpower, and is further constrained by current policy.

In 2007, the DHS Office of the Inspector General (OIG) conducted an inquiry into coordination challenges between CBP and ICE. The findings of the report highlight confusion amongst the respective agencies on the roles and responsibilities of each organization.[166] As recent as February 2012, the DHS OIG issued another report on a similar subject and found, "… operational challenges between U.S. Border Patrol and ICE HSI [Homeland Security Investigations] remain unresolved."[167] This systemic lack of unity of effort prevents the two organizations from applying the combined strength of their respective capabilities against threats on the border.

---

[166] *DHS' Progress In Addressing Coordination Challenges Between Customs and Border Protection and Immigration and Customs Enforcement*, 10.

[167] U.S. Department of Homeland Security, *Information Sharing on Foreign Nationals: Border Security (Redacted)* (Washington, DC: Officer of the Inspector General, February 2012), 17, http://www.oig.dhs.gov/assets/Mgmt/2012/OIGr_12-39_Feb12.pdf (accessed March 16, 2012).

One of these capabilities is the ability to collect, synthesize, and disseminate intelligence. According to the DHS OIG 2007 report, intelligence sharing between ICE and CBP was problematic; this problem continues today.[168] For example, ICE HSI shares information with CBP on a "need to know" basis; forcing the CBP to conduct its own intelligence collection activities. This results in a perception that ICE does not support CBP operations.[169] According to U.S. Army doctrine, "Intelligence and operations feed each other. Effective intelligence drives effective operations. Effective operations produce information, which generates more intelligence."[170] However, the current stove-piped analysis of intelligence between ICE HSI and CBP prevents a comprehensive picture of the threat along the Southwest Border.

In addition to the lack of a comprehensive intelligence capability between ICE and CBP, CBP lacks the ability to coordinate effectively air assets internally and with other agencies. For example, "to receive support for long-range air operations each sector chief and CBP headquarters must approve the use of air assets within each sector."[171] Adding complexity to the already divided air management system, "only the Border Patrol sector chief in the sending sector is required to approve air support, and the receiving sector may be notified as a courtesy."[172] Internally, the existing system does not provide sector chiefs situational awareness of all available

---

[168] *DHS' Progress In Addressing Coordination Challenges Between Customs and Border Protection and Immigration and Customs Enforcement*, 2.

[169] *Information Sharing on Foreign Nationals: Border Security (Redacted)*, 19.

[170] *Counterinsurgency*, 3-1.

[171] *DHS' Progress In Addressing Coordination Challenges Between Customs and Border Protection and Immigration and Customs Enforcement*, 11.

[172] Ibid.

assets in their areas of responsibility. Externally, the existing system is cumbersome, wreaked with bureaucracy, and is time consuming.[173]

Despite existing gaps between CPB and ICE, the CPB lacks the capability to fully control the two thousand mile long border with Mexico. In recent testimony to Congress, Mr. Richard Stana of the Government Accountability Office (GAO) stated, "… for fiscal year 2010…the Border Patrol reported achieving…operational control of…44 percent of the Southwest border."[174] At a cost of over three billion dollars for fiscal year 2010, this percentage of operational control over the Southwest Border is dismal; not to mention unsustainable in the current budget environment.[175] It would seem that the U.S. military could provide the capabilities necessary to fill this gaping hole in coverage, but JTF-North has capabilities shortfalls as well.

Currently there exist two gaps between JTF-North's current capabilities and the required capabilities needed to support the operations on the Southwest Border against the future threat environment: lack of existing capability, and policy limitations.[176] The lack of existing capability within JTF-North is due to the command having no assigned forces or authority to task units to provide support to CBP and ICE. In addition, current policy limits the ability of DOD forces in support of counterdrug operations by: mandating that a request for support come from a

---

[173] Ibid.

[174] House Committee on Homeland Security, *Securing Our Border-Operational Control and the Path Forward*, 112th Cong., 1st sess., 2011, 10-11, http://www.gpo.gov/fdsys/pkg/CHRG-112hhrg72215/pdf/CHRG-112hhrg72215.pdf (accessed March 21, 2012). The CBP defines operational control as, "the ability to detect, identify, classify, and then respond to and resolve illegal entries along our U.S. borders."

[175] *Securing Our Border-Operational Control and the Path Forward*, 11.

[176] *TRADOC Capabilities-Based Assessment (CBA) Version 3.1*, C-4.

counterdrug law enforcement agency; capping the amount of manpower associated with a CD mission; and limiting the amount of time military units can support a specific mission.[177]

Despite the much-needed support, JTF-North provides to both CBP and ICE operating on the border with Mexico, "JTF-North relies primarily on volunteer active duty and reserve components, as well as individual service members from all four branches of the Department of Defense for the execution of its homeland security support missions."[178] This reliance on "volunteer units" is due to the JTFs lack of assigned forces and tasking authority. According to the command's website, the most needed capabilities are medical, aviation, engineer, and mobile training teams. Further, the JTF is willing to pay most of the costs associated with the support provided by units.[179] This clearly indicates a supply and demand issue; where the demand is much greater than the supply.

Despite the gap in assigned forces and doctrine, DOD policy constrains the U.S. military in establishing a proactive and enduring approach to supporting Southwest Border operations. The Chairman of the Joint Chief of Staff, in accordance with the Stafford Act, instructed Geographical Combatant Commanders that, "… DOD CD support to a department or agency of the federal government must originate with an appropriate department or agency official responsible for CD activities."[180] In addition, the policy constrains DOD counterdrug support to, "… no more than 400 personnel…not exceeding 179 days for any one mission," without approval

---

[177] *DOD Counterdrug Support*, A-5 – A-6, A-9 – A-10.

[178] Joint Task Force North, Military Training Opportunities, http://www.jtfn northcom mil/ subpages/ mil_train.html (accessed February 21, 2012).

[179] Joint Task Force North, Military Training Opportunities, http://www.jtfn northcom.mil/ subpages/ mil_train.html (accessed February 21, 2012).

[180] *DOD Counterdrug Support*, A-9.

52

of the Secretary of Defense or President.[181] Taken as a whole, these three constraints make the assigning of forces to JTF–North impractical.

Without a change to JTF–North's existing capability and current DOD policy, the ability for U.S. military forces to meet the needs of both ICE and CBP today and in the future, places U.S. national security in jeopardy. United States Army doctrine provides insight on what it takes to secure borders and deny access into the country. Despite the current lack of assigned forces to JTF–North and constraints of DOD policy, solutions to overcome the challenges for safeguarding the Southwest Border are feasible.

Recommended Solution – Domestic Security Cooperation

The DOD and DHS must adopt a new approach along the Southwest Border to ensure the nation is fully prepared to deal with the "dangerous alternative." This new approach, called Domestic Security Cooperation (DSC), leverages the capabilities, experience, and capacity of the DOD to assist the interagency in building its own capacity. Based on the same fundamental principles (direct and indirect support) of Security Cooperation, used by other U.S. COCOMs across the globe, DSC focuses on the homeland.[182] Within this new framework, the DOD provides direct support through Security Force Assistance, logistics support, building intelligence cooperation between organizations, and military civic action. Indirectly, DOD provides support through training and education, combined exercises, and exchange programs.[183] By adopting DSC

---

[181] *DOD Counterdrug Support*, A-6.

[182] U.S. Department of Defense, *Foreign Internal Defense,* JP 3-22 (Washington, DC: Department of Defense, July 2010), I-8. Joint doctrine defines direct support as, "… operations [that] involve the use of US forces providing direct assistance to [host nation] civilian populace or military. Joint doctrine defines indirect support as, "… focus[ing] on building strong national infrastructures through economic and military capabilities that contribute to self-sufficiency."

[183] *Foreign Internal Defense,* I-8 – I-16.

as a new approach to homeland security and defense, the nation will truly harness the capabilities of both DOD and DHS to stand ready for the unknowns of tomorrow.

Applying DSC along the Southwest Border provides a solution to the incongruities between ICE and CBP. Today, the DOD has the capability to build capacity between both organizations to establish the organizational construct necessary for unity of effort and intelligence sharing, to streamline CBP air operations, and ten years of experience in both Iraq and Afghanistan to coach the interagency on how to extend operational control over vast swaths of terrain with limited forces. The remainder of this section will use the first three commodity areas of U.S. Army doctrine's DOTMLPF analysis to frame potential capability gap solutions. The acronym stands for: Doctrine, Organization, Training, Material, Leadership and Education, Personnel, and Facilities.[184] Further, policy will serve as an additional criterion to round out the assessment.

Doctrine

The U.S. Army defines doctrine as, "Fundamental principles by which the military forces or elements thereof guide their actions in support of national objectives. It is authoritative but requires judgment in application."[185] In addition, U.S. military doctrine serves as justification for designing force structure and resourcing the personnel equipment and training for that structure. While current doctrine provides fundamental principles related to DSCA, it does not adequately address DOD sustained support to domestic border security operations. Filling these doctrinal shortfalls requires a change in Joint and U.S. Army doctrine that accounts for the shortfalls in

---

[184] *TRADOC Capabilities-Based Assessment (CBA) Version 3.1*, 3, D-1.

[185] U.S. Department of the Army, *Operational Terms and Graphics*, FM 1-02 (Washington, DC: Department of the Army, September 2004), 1-65.

CBP and ICE capability and acknowledges the need for sustained U.S. military assistance to domestic security. To do this, DOD could update the *U.S. Army's Concept for Building Partnership Capacity* so that it includes concepts for support to the homeland; which it currently does not.[186] Additionally, the capabilities for border security outlined in FM 31-55, can serve as a framework for the potential capabilities required for building partnership capacity in the homeland.

Two of these capabilities include detection and response.[187] Each of these capabilities requires effective management and allocation of aircraft. To assist the CBP in providing seamless support to ICE, NORTHCOM, as a joint headquarters and a direct link to NORAD, can build capacity in air asset management by implementing the Air Tasking Order (ATO). The ATO is a, "… method used to task and disseminate to components, subordinate units, and command and control agencies those projected sorties/capabilities/forces to targets and specific missions."[188] This centralized approach to air asset management would break down the existing stove-piped system and ensure that crucial air assets, such as the MQ-9, support priority targets across the depth and breadth of the border.

Organization

Sound doctrine is of no value if an ineffective organizational construct exists within an institution. An organization, "… refers to the administrative and functional structures of the force

---

[186] U.S. Department of the Army, *U.S. Army's Concept for Building Partnership Capacity,* TRADOC PAM 525-8-4 (Washington, DC: Department of the Army, November 2011), D-1.2

[187] *Border Security/ Anti-Infiltration Operations,* 1-5 to 1-6.

[188] U.S. Department of Defense, *Command and Control of Joint Air Operations*, JP 3-56.1 (Washington, DC: Department of Defense, November 1994), GL-4.

as well as a culture that contributes to accomplish the force's mission."[189] Both U.S. Southern

Command (USSOUTHCOM) and U.S. Pacific Command (USPACOM) have a Joint Interagency

Task Force (JIATF) to unify efforts between the DOD and other U.S. government agencies.[190]

The JIATFs integrate DOD and federal law enforcement agency capabilities to combat illicit

trafficking, and include these agencies in the chain of command. Although focused in different

regions of the world, both organizations seek to unify efforts for a common cause. Underscoring

the effectiveness of a JIATF to unify desperate organizations, an author writing for the Institute

for National Strategic Studies lauded JIATF-South for, "… achiev[ing] unity of effort without

unity of command."[191] To build unity of effort along the Southwest Border, NORTHCOM can

build on the successes of both USSOUTHCOM and USPACOM, by establishing a JIATF for the

Southwest Border. Incorporating agencies such as ICE and CBP will further enhance the

comprehensive approach necessary for preventing narco-terrorism along the U.S.-Mexican

Border.

Key to preventing infiltration along the Southwest Border is timely and actionable

intelligence. Currently, ICE and CBP lack the collaborative framework to share intelligence, and

as a result do not have a sufficient targeting process. To overcome this gap, the JIATF should

organize a Joint Intelligence Coordination Cell (JICC). The purpose of the JICC is to identify

potential threats before they reach the nation's border and to disseminate the information to all

---

[189] Terrence K. Kelly and others, *A Stability Police Force for the United States: Justification and Options for Creating U.S. Capabilities* (Santa Monica, CA: Rand, 2009), 64.

[190] U.S. Pacific Command, Joint Interagency Task Force West, http://www.pacom.mil/web /site_pages/ %20directory/jiatfwest/jiatfwest.shtml; U.S. Southern Command, Joint Interagency Task Force South, http://www.jiatfs.southcom mil/index.aspx (accessed March 22, 2012).

[191] Evan Munsing and Christopher J. Lamb, "Joint Interagency Task Force-South: The Best Known, Least Understood Interagency Success," *Institute for National Strategic Perspectives,* no. 5 (June 2011), 77, http://www ndu.edu/inss/docuploaded/Strat%20Perspectives%205%20_%20Lamb-Munsing.pdf (accessed March 22, 2012).

agencies required for interdiction. Key to this effort is clarifying the role of ICE as the lead investigative arm of CBP. Additionally, adopting the U.S. Army targeting process, which focuses on linking objectives with effects, will further aid in accomplishing the overall unified vision.[192]

To ensure the needed support is available to both ICE and CBP, organizational change must occur within NORTHCOM, specifically JTF-North. Based on the required capabilities highlighted in the previous section, JTF-North requires assigned forces. These capabilities exist within the DOD. Under the existing U.S. Army force structure, regionally assigning a Maneuver Enhancement Brigade to JTF-North, meets the critical requirements for supporting ICE and CBP in border security and anti-infiltration operations.[193] However, this force will require additional training to both meet the needs of the interagency as well as operate within a homeland security environment.

Training

Any force assigned to JTF-North, such as a Maneuver Enhancement Brigade, requires specialized training to accomplish its mission. In addition to maintaining proficiency in tactics, techniques, and procedures (TTPs) for border security, and anti-infiltration operations, the military force will also require the capability to train CBP and ICE in response force operations, air asset management, and intelligence fusion. In addition, U.S. forces working with the interagency will require cultural and rules of engagement training. The constraints imposed by Posse Comitatus prevent active engagement by the U.S. military in law enforcement activities. However, FM 31-55 underscores a need for all the capabilities listed above for the effective

---

[192] *Counterinsurgency,* 5-29.

[193] U.S. Department of the Army, *Maneuver Enhancement Brigade Operations*, FM 3-90.31 (Washington, DC: February 2009), 2-2.

interdiction of cross-border infiltrators.[194] This training capacity should leverage the lessons learned in both Afghanistan and Iraq counterinsurgency operations.

These lessons learned will provide the answer for continued challenges facing ICE and CBP as they continue to wrestle with the depth and breadth of the Southwest Border. Although the combined manpower of ICE and CBP is more than a U.S. Army division, less than half of the natural border with Mexico is under U.S. operational control. However shocking this may be to some policy-makers, the U.S. military deals with this challenge daily. In places like Afghanistan and Iraq, the U.S. military continues to cover more ground with less Soldiers and Marines. To overcome this disadvantage, U.S. forces employ technology; including UASs, ground sensors, and robust networks to support information sharing. This real-world knowledge and experience, implemented through combined training exercises, education, and exchange programs, will assist the interagency in better operational planning and force allocation.

Policy

The final requirement for solving the gap in capabilities is changing military and national policy. The foundation of DOD support to law enforcement agencies within the U.S. stems from the Stafford Act. This statutory constraint requires that a formal request for support come from a local or state entity. Nested with this constraint, DOD support along the Southwest Border hinges on requests for support from law enforcement agencies and limits the number of service-members and time afforded to a specific mission. These constraints currently prevent changes to doctrine, organization, and training, because do so is counter-intuitive. Therefore, a change to both national and joint policy is required to ease restrictions that prevent federal authorities from effectively

---

[194] *Border Security/ Anti-Infiltration Operations,* 3-10.

using all national resources to combat national-level problems, such as securing the nation's borders.

Conclusion

The emerging threats to the nation and the shortfalls in the capabilities to counter those threats, highlights the need for a different approach to homeland security and defense. Using the increased violence on the Southwest Border and potential alliance of Mexican-based TCOs and extremist groups as a possible future threat to national security, the basis of this analysis attempts to highlight the inadequacy of the current approach to homeland security and defense. The current approach hinges on the cooperation between ICE, CBP, and assistance provided by JTF-North. However, the lack of cooperation and capability between the three organizations prevents an effective deterrent against the potential tidal wave of instability brewing south of the border. To reverse the tide requires a comprehensive approach; including unity of effort, increased intelligence sharing, effective air asset management, and use of sensors and manpower to cover the more than two thousand miles of border with Mexico. Leveraging the U.S. military's capacity and capability can fill the void and provide the necessary capability and capacity to enhance interagency efforts.

Cooperation between federal law enforcement and the U.S. military stems back to the post-Civil War Reconstruction Era. With limited domestic policy constraints, such as Posse Comitatus, the civil-military cooperation during this period was very effective at quelling internal terrorist threats such as the Klu Klux Klan. However, as the U.S. took on a greater international role following the Spanish American War, it was evident that the nation needed institutions that had the capacity and authority to provide for homeland security.

As the nation matured, federal law enforcement agencies such as the FBI and the USSS took on a greater role for homeland security; as the U.S. military became the sole provider of homeland defense. These roles continued to solidify through WWI, and WWII. However, the onset of the Cold War saw a shift in the roles of federal law enforcement. No longer burdened by international threats to the homeland, they began focusing on internal issues such as gang violence, organized crime, and popular uprisings. Why not? The U.S. military, along with two large oceans, provided the necessary defense against the existential threat of the U.S.S.R. In the last decade of the 20th century, a U.S. led coalition ousted Saddam Hussein's army from Kuwait and reinforced the existing approach to homeland security and defense. However, the approach, carried through the 1990s, ensured that the nation was ill prepared for the attacks carried out by Al Qaeda on 9/11.

After the Twin Towers fell, the nation's leaders realized that the status quo approach to homeland security and defense no longer applied. President Bush reformed the Executive Branch and created the DHS. The DOD provided a seemingly more collaborative role in homeland security by creating joint doctrine for DSCA. However, in doing so the DOD further widened the civil-military gap and made it more difficult to apply the full weight of military assistance against emerging threats within the homeland. Despite this, trends in the operational environment provide an opportunity to once again relook the approach to homeland security and defense. Increased collaboration and cooperation between the U.S. military and DHS is the answer to problems facing the nation today.

Arguing for greater cooperation and interoperability between the U.S. military and its interagency partners is not a new idea. In order to strengthen national defense, President Barack Obama's *National Security Strategy 2010* states, "[The U.S. Government must improve] the integration of skills and capabilities within our military and civilian institutions…and must

60

build…capacity in key areas where we [the U.S. military and interagency] fall short."[195] In addition, the *National Defense Strategy 2008* directs the U.S. military to, "… [Work] to improve understanding and harmonize best practices amongst interagency partners… [and] increase our collective abilities to defend the homeland."[196] The recently published *Quadrennial Homeland Security Review Report 2010* echoes the same theme of U.S. military and interagency cooperation as the *National Security Strategy 2010* and *National Defense Strategy 2008*.[197] All three documents clearly state the strategic end state in regards to the cooperation of the U.S. military and interagency in providing homeland security, but do not describe the ways.

The way is through DSC, but to ensure the success of this powerful combination, the commander of NORTHCOM needs sufficient resources for the task. These resources come in the form of assigned units and their inherent capabilities. By assigning units, the NORTHCOM commander has options available to establish a robust DSC plan (DSCP) that builds capacity through direct and indirect support to the interagency, and responds to unforeseen contingencies within the homeland.[198] This new approach will not only benefit the DHS, but will also benefit

---

[195] President, *National Security Strategy 2010* (Washington, DC: May 2010), 14.

[196] *National Defense Strategy 2008*, 18.

[197] *Quadrennial Homeland Security Review Report*, 36. The QHSR identifies four lines of operation to "mature and strengthen the Homeland Security Enterprise." One of the four lines of effort, "Foster Unity of Effort", includes a supporting objective of "further enhance the military-homeland security relationship."

[198] *Department of Defense Dictionary of Military and Associated Terms*, 420. The planning, applied at the Geographic Combatant Command level, defined as, "All Department of Defense interactions with foreign defense establishments to build defense relationships that promote specific US security interests, develop allied and friendly military capabilities for self-defense and multinational operations, and provide US forces with peacetime and contingency access to a host nation."

the U.S. Army by providing real-world application of Department of Defense Directive (DODD) 3000.05.[199]

Although this analysis focused on the interaction between NORTHCOM, CBP, and ICE as applied to the Southwest Border, it can also apply to other interagency organizations operating within the homeland. Further research is necessary to understand maritime coordination between the U.S. Coast Guard and CBP, efforts along the Northern Border with Canada, and U.S. military assistance to the Drug Enforcement Agency (DEA). Through this continued research and synthesis of information, perhaps something new can be created.

---

[199] U.S. Department of Defense, *Military Support for Stability, Security, Transition, and Reconstruction (SSTR) Operations*, Directive 3000.05, November 28, 2005, 2. DODD 3000.05 directs the U.S. military to consider Stability Operations just as important as Combat Operations.

BIBLIOGRAPHY

Books

Baker, James E. *In the Common Defense: National Security Law for Perilous Times.* New York: Cambridge University Press, 2007.

Cooper, Christopher, and Robert Block. *Disaster: Hurricane Katrina and the Failure of Homeland Security.* New York: Henry Holt and Company, 2006.

Dollman, Everett Carl. *Pure Strategy: Power and Principles in the Space and Information Age.* New York: Frank Cass-Taylor & Francis, 2005.

Jeffreys-Jones, Rhodri. *The FBI: A History.* New Haven, CT: Yale University Press, 2007.

Johnson, Paul. *A History of the American People.* New York: Harper Collins Publishers, 1997.

Kelly, Terrence K., Seth G. Jones, James E. Barnett II, Keith Crane, Robert C. Davis, and Carl Jensen. *A Stability Police Force for the United States: Justification and Options for Creating U.S. Capabilities.* Santa Monica, CA: Rand, 2009.

Lansford, Tom, Robert J. Pauly, Jr., and Jack Covarrubias. *To Protect and Defend: US Homeland Security Policy.* Burlington, VT: Ashgate Publishing Company, 2006.

Lapp, John Augustus. *Supplement to 1917, to Lapp's Important Federal Laws.* Indianapolis, IN: B.F. Bowen & Company, 1917. http://books.google.com/books/ (accessed December 14, 2011).

Mahon, John K. *History of the Militia and the National Guard.* New York: Macmillan Publishing Company, 1983.

Mallory, John A. "The Militia." In *Compiled Statutes of the United States: Supplement 1903.* St. Paul, MN: West Publishing Company, 190. http://books.google.com/ (accessed December 14, 2011).

Maxwell, Bruce. *Homeland Security: A Documentary History.* Washington, DC: CQ Press, 2004.

Reynolds, Paul Davidson. *A Primer on Theory Construction.* Needham Heights, MA: Allyn and Bacon, 1971.

Swain, Richard M. *Lucky War: Third Army in Desert Storm.* Washington, DC: U.S. Army Center of Military History, 1997.

Turabian, Kate L. *A Manual for Writers of Research Papers, Theses, and Dissertations.* 7th ed. Chicago: University of Chicago Press, 2007.

Wade, Wyn Craig. *The Fiery Cross: The Klu Klux Klan in America.* London: Simon and Schuster, 1987.

Journal Articles

Gorman, Martin, and Alexander Konrad. "A Goldwater-Nichols Act for the U.S. Government: Institutionalizing the Interagency Process." *Joint Force Quarterly*, no. 39 (4th Quarter

2005). https://digitalndulibrary.ndu.edu/cdm4/document.php?CISOROOT=/ndupress& CISOPTR=19198&REC=2 (accessed September 16, 2011).

Killebrew, Bob, and Jennifer Bernal. "Crime Wars: Gangs, Cartels and U.S. National Security." Center for New American Security, September 2010.

Killibrew, Robert. "Criminal Insurgency in the Americas and Beyond." *Prism* 2, no. 3 (June 2011).http://www.ndu.edu/press/lib/images/prism2-3/Prism_33-52_Killebrew.pdf (accessed January 30, 2012)

Manwaring, Max. *A "New" Dynamic in the Western Hemisphere Security Environment: The Mexican Zetas and other Private Armies.* Carlisle, PA: Strategic Studies Institute, 2009. http://www.strategicstudiesinstitute.army.mil/pdffiles/PUB940.pdf (accessed January 24, 2012).

Munsing, Evan, and Christopher J. Lamb. "Joint Interagency Task Force-South: The Best Known, Least Understood Interagency Success." *Institute for National Strategic Perspectives,* no. 5 (June 2011). http://www.ndu.edu/inss/docuploaded/ Strat%20Perspectives%205%20_%20Lamb-Munsing.pdf (accessed March 22, 2012).

Stanton, Louise. *The Civilian-Military Divide: Obstacles to the Integration of Intelligence in the United States.* Santa Barbara, CA: Praeger Security International, 2009.

Sullivan, John P., and Adam Elkus. "Plazas for Profit: Mexico's Criminal Insurgency" *Small Wars Journal*, (April, 2009). http://smallwarsjournal.com/blog/ journal / docs-temp/232-sullivan.pdf?q=mag/docs-temp/232-sullivan.pdf (accessed January 27, 2012).

Turbiville, Graham H. "US-Mexican Border Security: Civil-Military Cooperation." *Military Review* 79, no. 4 (July-August 1999). http://calldp.leavenworth.army.mil/call_pub.html (accessed September 6, 2011).

Government Documents

Beittel, June S. *Mexico's Drug Trafficking Organizations: Source and Scope of the Rising Violence.* CRS Report for Congress R41576. Washington, DC: Congressional Research Service, January 7, 2011. http://assets.opencrs.com/rpts/R41576_20110107.pdf (accessed January 22, 2012).

Beittel, June S. *Mexico's Drug Related Violence.* CRS Report for Congress R40582. Washington, DC: Congressional Research Service, May 27, 2009. http://www.fas.org/sgp/crs/row/ R40582.pdf (accessed January 22, 2012).

Benjamin, Daniel. "Al Qaeda and Its Affiliates." Remarks to the New America Foundation Conference, Washington, DC, April 27, 2011. http://www.state.gov/j/ct/rls/ rm/2011/161895.htm (accessed February 13, 2012)

Bjelopera, Jerome P. *American Jihadist Terrorism: Combating a Complex Threat.* CRS Report for Congress R41416. Washington, DC: Congressional Research Service, November 15, 2011. http://www.fas.org/sgp/crs/terror/R41416.pdf (accessed February 12, 2012).

Bolkcom, Christopher, Lloyd DeSerisy, and Lawrence Kapp. *Homeland Security: Establishment and Implementation of the Northern Command.* CRS Report for Congress RS21322.

Washington, DC: Congressional Research Service, May 14, 2003. http://www.fas.org/man/crs/ RS21322.pdf (accessed October 20, 2011).

Bonds, Timothy M., Myron Hura, and Thomas-Durell Young. *Enhancing Army Joint Force Headquarters Capabilities*. Santa Monica, CA: Rand, 2010.

Bowman, Steve, and James Crowhurst. *Homeland Security: Evolving Roles and Missions for United States Northern Command*. CRS Report for Congress RS21322. Washington, DC: Congressional Research Service, November 16, 2006. http://www.fas.org/man/crs/ RS21322.pdf (accessed October 20, 2011).

Builder, Carl H. *Measuring the Leverage: Assessing Military Contributions to Drug Interdiction*. Santa Monica, CA: Rand, 1993.

Center for Strategic and International Studies. *Beyond Goldwater-Nichols: Defense Reform for a New Strategic Era, Phase 1 Report*. Washington DC: Center for Strategic and International Studies, March 2004. http://www.csis.org (accessed July 15, 2011).

Davis, Lynn E., David E. Mosher, Richard R. Brennan, Michael D. Greenberg, K. Scott McMahon, and Charles W. Yost. *Army Forces for Homeland Security*. Santa Monica, CA: Rand, 2004. http://www.rand.org/pubs/monographs/2004/RAND_MG221.pdf (accessed October 1, 2011).

Executive Order no. 13581. *Blocking Property of Transnational Criminal Organizations*. July 24, 2011. http://www.gpo.gov/fdsys/pkg/DCPD-201100523/pdf/DCPD-201100523.pdf (accessed January 25, 2012).

Finklea, Kristin, William Krouse and Marc Rosenblum. *Southwest Border Violence: Issues in Identifying and Measuring Spillover Violence*. CRS Report for Congress R41075. Washington, DC: Congressional Research Service, June 9, 2011. http://www.fas.org/sgp/crs/homesec/R41075.pdf (accessed September 15, 2011).

Haddal, Chad C. *Border Security: The Role of the U.S. Border Patrol*. CRS Report for Congress RL32562. Washington, DC: Congressional Research Service, August 11, 2010. http://www.fas.org/sgp/crs/homesec/RL32562.pdf (accessed March 12, 2012).

Krepinevich, Andrew, and Robert O. Work. *A New US Global Defense Posture for the Second Transoceanic Era*. Washington, DC: Center for Strategic and Budgetary Assessments, 2007. http:// www.csbaonline.org/wp-content/uploads/2011/02/2007.04.20-New-Global-Defense-Posture.pdf (accessed November 30, 2011).

McCaffrey, Barry R. "Statement for the Record Submitted by General Barry R. McCaffrey (USA, Ret)." U.S. House of Representatives Committee on Homeland Security Subcommittee on Oversight, Investigations, and Management, Hearing on: "A Call to Action: Narco-Terrorism's Threat to the U.S. Southern Border." http://homeland.house.gov/sites/ homeland.house.gov/files/ Testimony%20McCaffrey.pdf (accessed February 15, 2012).

National Commission on Terrorist Attacks. *9/11 Commission Report*. New York: Barnes and Noble Publishing, 2004.

National Immigration Forum. "Backgrounder: Southwest Border Security Operations." Washington, DC: National Immigration Forum, December 2010. http://www.immigrationforum.org/images/uploads/SouthwestBorderSecurityOperations.pdf (accessed March 12, 2012).

Pew Research Center, "Public's Priorities for 2010: Economy, Jobs, Terrorism." Washington, DC: Pew Research Center for the People and the Press, January 25, 2010. http://www.people-press.org/files/legacy-pdf/584.pdf (accessed February 11, 2012).

Rodham-Clinton, Hillary. "Remarks with Mexican Foreign Secretary Patricia Espinosa." Speech given at Mexico City, Mexico, March 25, 2009. http://www.state.gov/secretary /rm/ 2009a/03/120905.htm (accessed January 30, 2012).

Seelke, Clare Ribando and Kristin M. Finklea. *U.S.-Mexican Security Cooperation: The Mérida Initiative and Beyond.* CRS Report for Congress R41349. Washington, DC: Congressional Research Service, August 15, 2011. http://www.fas.org/sgp /crs/row/R41349.pdf (accessed February March 1, 2012).

Shirk, David A. "Transnational Crime, U.S. Border Security, and the War on Drugs in Mexico." Delivered to the House of Representatives Sub-Committee on Oversight, Investigations, and Management, Chairman: Hon. Michael McCaul, March 31, 2011. http://homeland.house.gov/sites/homeland.house.gov/files/Testimony%20Shirk.pdf (accessed March 21, 2012).

Shepherd, Scott, and Steve Bowman. *Homeland Security: Establishment and Implementation of the United States Northern Command.* CRS Report for Congress RS21322. Washington, DC: Congressional Research Service, February 10, 2005. http://www.fas.org/man/crs/ RS21322.pdf (accessed October 20, 2011).

U.S. Congress. House. Committee on Homeland Security. *Securing Our Border-Operational Control and the Path Forward.* 112th Cong., 1st sess. February 15, 2011. http://www.gpo.gov/fdsys/pkg/CHRG-112hhrg72215/ pdf/CHRG-112hhrg72215.pdf (accessed March 21, 2012).

U.S. Congress. House. Committee on Homeland Security. *U.S. Homeland Security Role in the Mexican War Against Drug Cartels.* 112th Cong., 1st sess. March 31, 2011. http://www.hsdl.org/?view&did=7774 (accessed April 11, 2012).

U.S. Congress. Senate. Committee on Homeland Security and Governmental Affairs. *Nine Years After 9/11: Confronting the Terrorist Threat to the Homeland.* 111th Cong., 2nd sess., September 22, 2010. http://www.hsgac.senate.gov/hearings/nine-years-after-9/11-confronting-the-terrorist-threat-to-the-homeland (accessed February 11, 2012).

U.S. Department of Homeland Security. *DHS' Progress In Addressing Coordination Challenges Between Customs and Border Protection and Immigration and Customs Enforcement.* Washington, DC: Office of Inspector General, April 2007. http://www.oig.dhs.gov/ assets/Mgmt /OIG_07-38_Apr07.pdf (accessed March 14, 2012).

U.S. Department of Homeland Security. *ICE Investigations: Mission Roles in Multi-Agency Areas of Responsibility.* Washington, DC: Immigration and Customs Enforcement, August 2007. http://www.fbiic.gov/public/2008/may/ICE_Mission_Roles.pdf (accessed March 13, 2012).

U.S. Department of Homeland Security. *Information Sharing on Foreign Nationals: Border Security (Redacted).* Washington, DC: Officer of the Inspector General, February 2012. http://www.oig.dhs.gov/assets/Mgmt/2012/OIGr_12-39_Feb12.pdf (accessed March 16, 2012).

U.S. Department of Homeland Security. *National Border Patrol Strategy*. Washington, DC: U.S. Customs and Border Protection, September 2004.

U.S. Department of Homeland Security. *National Response Framework*. Washington, DC: U.S. Department of Homeland Security, January 2008.

U.S. Department of Homeland Security. *Protecting America: U.S. Customs and Border Protection 2005-2010 Strategic Plan*. Washington, DC: Customs and Border Protection, May 2005. http://www.aapa-ports.org/files/PDFs/CBP_5year_StrategicPlan.pdf (accessed March 22, 2012).

U.S. Department of Homeland Security. *Robert T. Stafford Disaster Relief and Emergency Assistance Act, as Amended, and Related Authorities*. Washington, DC: Federal Emergency Management Agency, 2007. http://www.fema.gov/pdf/about/stafford_act.pdf (accessed December 30, 2011).

U.S. Department of Homeland Security. *Secure Border, Safe Travel, Legal Trade: U.S. Customs and Border Protection Fiscal Year 2009-2014 Strategic Plan*. Washington, DC: Customs and Border Protection, July, 2009. http://www.cbp.gov/linkhandler/cgov/about/mission/strategic_plan_09_14.ctt/strategic_plan_09_14.pdf (accessed February 26, 2012).

U.S. Department of Homeland Security. "Snapshot: A Summary of CBP facts and figures." Washington, DC: U.S. Customs and Border Protection, February 2012. http://www.cbp.gov/linkhandler/ cgov/about/accomplish/cbp_snapshot.ctt/snapshot.pdf (accessed March 12, 2012).

U.S. Department of Homeland Security. *Surveillance Lesson Plan Field Operations Training Plan*. Washington, DC: Immigration and Customs Enforcement, February 2011. www.michiganimmigrant.org/advocate_library/ice_training.../file (accessed April 11, 2012)

U.S. Department of Homeland Security. *U.S. Immigration and Customs Enforcement Strategic Plan FY 2010-2014*. Washington, DC: Immigration and Customs Enforcement, June 2010. http://www.ice.gov/about/overview/ (accessed March 15, 2012).

U.S. Department of Justice. *National Drug Threat Assessment 2011*. Washington, DC: National Drug Intelligence Center, 2011. http://www.justice.gov/ndic/pubs44/44849/44849p.pdf (accessed January 22, 2012).

U.S. Department of Justice. *The Evolution of Terrorism Since 9/11*, by Lauren B. O'Brien. Washington, DC: Federal Bureau of Investigation, 2011. http://www.fbi.gov/stats-services/publications /law-enforcement-bulletin/september-2011/the-evolution-of-terrorism-since-9-11 (accessed February 11, 2012).

U.S. Department of State. *Post-Conflict Reconstruction Essential Tasks*. Washington DC: Office of Reconstruction and Stabilization, April 2005. http://www.state.gov/documents/organization/161791.pdf (accessed September 6, 2011).

U.S. Government Accountability Office. *Hurricane Katrina: Better Plans and Exercises Needed to Guide the Military's Response to Catastrophic Natural Disasters*. Washington, DC: Government Accountability Office, 2006. http://www.gao.gov/new.items/d06643.pdf (accessed February 13, 2012).

U.S. President. *National Security Strategy 1995.* Washington, DC: February 1995.
http://www.au.af.mil/au/awc/awcgate/nss/nss-95.pdf (accessed December 13, 2011).

U.S. President. *National Security Strategy 2010.* Washington, DC: May 2010.

U.S. President. *National Strategy for Counterterrorism.* Washington, DC: June 2011.
http://www.whitehouse.gov/sites/default/files/counterterrorism_strategy.pdf (accessed
February 14, 2012).

U.S. President. "Overview of the Foreign Narcotics Kingpin Designation Act." Washington, DC:
Office of the Press Secretary, April 15, 2009. http://www.whitehouse.gov/the_press_
office/Fact-Sheet-Overview-of-the-Foreign-Narcotics-Kingpin-Designation-Act/
(accessed January 24, 2012).

U.S. President. Budget. "Historical Tables." *Budget of the United States Government, Fiscal Year
2005.* Washington, DC: Government Printing Office, 2004. http://www.gpoaccess.gov
/usbudget/ fy05/pd /hist.pdf (accessed December 12, 2011).

Winnefeld, James A. "Statement before the House Armed Services Committee." March 30, 2011.
http://www.northcom.mil/Docs/2011%20NORAD%20and%20USNORTHCOM%20
Posture% 20Statement %20(HASC%20Final).pdf (accessed February 21, 2012).

Military Publications

Letcher, Stephen A. "Reorganizing to Meet the Homeland Security Challenges of 2010."
Monograph, School of Advanced Military Studies, Command and General Staff College,
2003. http://cgsc.cdmhost.com/cdm/singleitem/collection/p4013coll3/id/38/rec/3.

U.S. Department of the Army. *Afghanistan Study Group: Operational Campaign Plan.* Fort
Leavenworth, KS: Command and General Staff College, 2009.

U.S. Department of the Army. *Border Security/ Anti-Infiltration Operations.* FM 31-55.
Washington, DC: Department of the Army, 1968. http://www.ebookdb.org/reading
/G216621AG67348743A2B7F69/Border-Securityanti-infiltration-Operations (accessed
February 26, 2012).

U.S. Department of the Army. *Counterinsurgency.* FM 3-24. Washington, DC: U.S. Department
of the Army, December 2006.

U.S. Department of the Army. *Maneuver Enhancement Brigade Operations.* FM 3-90.31
Washington, DC: February 2009.

U.S. Department of the Army. *The Operations Process.* FM 5-0. Washington, DC: U.S.
Department of the Army, March 2010.

U.S. Department of the Army. *Operational Terms and Graphics.* FM 1-02 Washington, DC:
Department of the Army, September 2004.

U.S. Department of the Army. *Stability Operations.* FM 3-07. Washington, DC: U.S. Department
of the Army, October 2008.

U.S. Department of the Army. *The Army.* FM 1. Washington, DC: U.S. Department of the Army,
June 2005.

U.S. Department of the Army. *The U.S. Army Concept for Building Partner Capacity*. TRADOC Pam 525-8-4. Washington, DC: U.S. Department of the Army, November 2011.

U.S. Department of the Army, *The United Stated Army Operating Concept 2016-2028*. TRADOC PAM 525-3-1. Washington, DC: Department of the Army, August 19, 2010. http://www.tradoc.army.mil/tpubs/pams/tp525-3-1.pdf (accessed February 18, 2012).

U.S. Department of the Army. *TRADOC Capabilities-Based Assessment (CBA) Version 3.1*. Fort Monroe, VA: Training and Doctrine Command, May 10, 2010.

U.S. Department of Defense. *Civil Support*. JP 3-28. Washington, DC: Department of Defense, September 14, 2007.

U.S. Department of Defense. *Command and Control of Joint Air Operations*. JP 3-56.1. Washington, DC: Department of Defense, November 1994.

U.S. Department of Defense. *DOD Counterdrug Support*. CJCSI 3710.10B, January 26, 2007. http://www.dtic.mil/cjcs_directives/cdata/unlimit/3710_01.pdf (accessed December 28, 2011).

U.S. Department of Defense. *Defense Science Board 2003 Summer Study of DOD Roles and Missions in Homeland Security*. Vol. 1. Washington, DC: Office of the Under Secretary of Defense for Acquisition, Technology, and Logistics, 2003.

U.S. Department of Defense. *Department of Defense Dictionary of Military and Associated Terms*. JP 1-02. Washington DC: U.S. Department of Defense, April 12, 2001.

U.S. Department of Defense, *Doctrine for the Armed Forces of the United States*. JP-1. Washington, DC: Department of Defense, May 2, 2007.

U.S. Department of Defense. *Foreign Internal Defense*. JP 3-22. Washington, DC: Department of Defense, July 2010.

U.S. Department of Defense. *Joint Operating Environment*. Washington, DC: Department of Defense, 2008. http://www.jfcom.mil/newslink/storyarchive/2008/JOE2008.pdf (accessed February 15, 2012).

U.S. Department of Defense. *Joint Operating Environment*. Washington, DC: Department of Defense, 2010.

U.S. Department of Defense. *Military Support for Stability, Security, Transition, and Reconstruction (SSTR) Operations*. Directive 3000.05. November 28, 2005.

U.S. Department of Defense. *The History of the Unified Command Plan 1946-1999*. Washington, DC: Office of the Chairman of the Joint Chiefs of Staff, 2003.

U.S. Department of Defense. *Joint Counterdrug Operations*. JP 3-07.4. Washington DC: U.S. Department of Defense, June 13, 2007.

U.S. Department of Defense. *2008 National Defense Strategy*. Washington DC: Office of the Secretary of Defense, June 2008.

U.S. Department of Defense. *Quadrennial Defense Review Report*. Washington, DC: Department of Defense September 30, 2001. http://www.dod.gov/pubs/qdr2001.pdf (accessed February 11, 2012).

Newspaper Articles

Brayman, Gail. "USNORTHCOM contributes pandemic flu contingency expertise to trilateral workshop." *northcom.mil/news*, April 14, 2008. http://www.northcom.mil/news /2008/041408.html (accessed February 14, 2012).

British Broadcasting Corporation. "Q&A: Mexico's drug-related violence." *BBC.com,* January 25, 2012. http://www.bbc.co.uk/news/world-latin-america-10681249 (accessed February 18, 2012).

Carrasco, Armando. "2nd Intel Battalion Supports Border Patrol in South Texas." May 2, 2011, http://www.marines.mil/unit/iimef/Pages/2ndIntelBorderPatrol.aspx (accessed February 21, 2012)

Garamone, Jim. "Pace Proposes Interagency Goldwater-Nichols Act." *American Forces Press Service*, September 7, 2004. http://www.defense.gov/news/newsarticle.aspx?id=25384 (accessed September 16, 2011).

Gibson, Dave. "The U.S. Military should be used to defend our border with Mexico." *Examiner.com*, January 28, 2010, http://www.examiner.com/immigration-reform-in-national/the-u-s-military-should-be-used-to-defend-our-border-with-mexico#ixzz1n4k6EF91 (accessed February 21, 2012).

Holman, Brent. "US Customs and Border Protection widens air role." *Professional Pilot Magazine.* February 2009, http://www.propilotmag.com/archives/2009/ Feb09/A2_USCustoms_p1.html (accessed April 10, 2012).

Phares, Walid. "The Ashburn Jihadist Signals a Greater Danger." *WashtingtonTimes.com*, November 10, 2010, http://www.washingtontimes.com/news/2010/nov/5/the-fbis-arrest-of-farooque-ahmed-of-ashburn-va-fo/?page=1 (accessed September 15, 2011).

Rockwell, Mark. "JTF North to aid CBP in NM and AZ in February." *GSNmagazine.com*, February 10, 2012, http://www.gsnmagazine.com/node/25619 (accessed February 21, 2012).

Taylor, Jared. "U.S. Agents Find Rocket Launcher Near Mexico Border." *REUTERS.com*, September 14, 2011. http://www.reuters.com/article/2011/09/14/us-usa-mexico-weapons-idUSTRE78D7HK20110914?feedType=RSS&feedName=domesticNews (accessed January 27, 2012).